Promise in the Cornfield

Madlyn Hamblin

Pacific Press Publishing Association
Boise, Idaho
Oshawa, Ontario, Canada

Edited by Randy Maxwell
Designed by Tim Larson
Cover by Jack Pardue
Type set in 10/12 Century Schoolbook

Library of Congress Catalog Card Number: 88-61525

ISBN 0-8163-0777-6

89 90 91 92 93 • 5 4 3 2 1

Lovingly Dedicated To

My husband, Ray, whose encouragement and financial generosity made this book possible.

Acknowledgements

Kenneth Livesay	for putting Chessie and me together.
Marilyn Mabrey	whose research and organizational skills help knit the raveled facets of Chessie's life together.
Loretta Montgomery	A gracious typist who volunteered many hours transcribing original taped conversations.
Evelyn Gates	The lifesaver who transcribed the final draft onto computer disc.
Mother and Dad (Virgil and Marian Lewis)	without whose inherited talents and abilities, this dream may never have been realized.

Table of Contents

For the Reader

This is the story of a woman who cares deeply about destitute and unloved children. The hows and whys are dramatic and in some instances miraculous.

Growing up as the child of a poor sharecropper, Chessie Harris soon discovered the pain of prejudice. Her brushes with bigotry, however, only served to intensify her drive to make poor children smile. She wanted them to feel good about themselves. She yearned for the same advantages white people had. Not only for herself, but for all the little ones she saw daily who looked so dirty and hungry.

Guided by compassion and totally committed to helping others, Chessie Harris has spent most of her life working to accomplish her mission.

She saw a need.

She set a goal.

And with the help of God, Chessie and her family have cared for more than 900 children to date.

Chessie's most valuable character trait is caring, and she has the uncanny ability to pull this virtue out of other people too. She's "Mama Harris" to anyone who needs her, and her door is always open.

Chessie says, "In this day and age, what's needed to raise children is enormous energy, willingness to do battle for them on all fronts, and unflagging optimism in their possibilities."

This positive attitude is linked with a steel-like determination to succeed that complements Chessie's willingness to sacrifice her own pleasures and needs for those who are less fortunate.

Chessie's refusal to take No for an answer when searching for ways to fulfill her dreams contributes to her uniqueness. She's often had to fight against seemingly insurmountable odds to care for needy human beings.

"Everything I learned to do and do well, I learned on my knees and from my Bible," Chessie declares. "I've always depended on God!" The verse of Scripture that has been the driving force behind Chessie's work is Isaiah 58:7 where it says, "Bring right into your own homes those who are helpless, poor and destitute" (LB).

Bringing nearly naked and unloved youngsters into her home is what Chessie Harris has been doing for more than three decades. And finally, she is getting the national recognition she deserves. In October of 1987, she was chosen as an outstanding American woman by *Women's Day* magazine. This honor, along with hundreds of others, has overwhelmed the unassuming "miracle worker of Alabama." "I don't know what all the fuss is about," Chessie says. "I just did what needed to be done."

Chessie has always been a crusader against apathy, and though she didn't choose her lot in life, she did choose to use her unique gifts and abilities to make a difference in the lives of little children. And it is her earnest desire that this story will inspire you to make a difference in the lives of those around you who may be in need.

Chessie has given much in the past. And she continues to achieve significant results whenever she puts her mind to a project. But her greatest gift is to the future—precious lives salvaged from life's scrapheap and given again to bless and contribute to the very world that once shunned them. We thank you, Chessie, for your gift of love.

And, to God be the glory.

—Madlyn Lewis Hamblin

Chapter 1

The Meaning of
Deprivation—1950

*I was an hungered, and ye gave me meat: I was thirsty, and ye gave
me drink: I was a stranger, and ye took me in: naked, and ye clothed
me: I was sick, and ye visited me. . . . And the King shall answer
and say unto them, Verily I say unto you, Inasmuch as ye have done
it unto one of the least of these my brethren, ye have done it unto me
(Matthew 25:35-40).*

Chessie Harris guided her 1949 Buick down the ghetto
streets of Huntsville, Alabama.

"Lord, have mercy," she prayed as she peered out the window of her car. "Why are so many children on the streets this
time of day?" she wondered. "Why aren't they in school?"

She watched the parade of humanity move about, con-
gregate, linger in doorways and front yards. She passed
dilapidated shanties and tin-top shacks. Old sofas and chairs
spilling cotton and straw sat forlornly on lopsided porches.
There were rusty, beat-up cars resting on flattened tires
among mountains of junk scattered about in some yards.
People were living in condemned houses that had long ago
been boarded up. And on every street the same scene was
repeated again and again—ragged, dirty, shoeless little waifs
existing in a cesspool of poverty.

Chessie hadn't gone far before she spotted a small boy shuf-
fling into a corner market. Fascinated by his disheveled ap-
pearance, she stopped her car, got out, and went into the store.

Chessie watched as the child spoke to the man behind the meat counter. In a few moments the butcher tossed the youngster a package, which he clutched tightly in his skinny arms.

Chessie followed the child at a distance so she wouldn't frighten him. Stealing away behind the store, she saw a little fire of sticks and grass burning in a #10 tin can. Unwrapping the package, the boy withdrew the scraps of raw meat, put them over the can, and stood back to watch them cook.

At this point Chessie stepped forward and asked, "What are you doing, Sonny? Cooking?"

He looked up at her, surprise showing in his eyes.

"Yes'm," he said. "I 'tended I had a dog, so the man gave me this." He pointed to the meager scraps. "I ain't had nothin' to eat since day 'fore yesterday."

The words pierced Chessie's heart, and her eyes were soon brimming with tears.

"Come on, Son. Mama Harris will take you to get somethin' to eat." Chessie placed her arm around the lad and ushered him to her car. She drove to a nearby restaurant and ordered a meal for her new friend. Few words were spoken as the hungry child consumed a large plateful of fried chicken, mashed potatoes and gravy, and cole slaw. But with some gentle and persistent prodding, Chessie soon learned that the child did not have anyone looking after him. Most of the time he fended for himself—alone.

All too soon the meal was completed, and though it hurt her heart to do so, Chessie knew she had to take the child back where she had found him. After braking to a stop in front of the same market where she first spotted him, Chessie hugged the little boy tightly and said an emotional goodbye.

Later that evening she told her husband, George, about the young lad. "I did what I could for him right then," Chessie said. "But I know that's not enough. The child needs someone to love him and take care of him. It just hurts my heart."

At fifty-three, Chessie was no stranger to hardship and the pain of discrimination. Although she had a good job as the food service director of Oakwood College in Huntsville, and a flourishing marriage that had been blessed with five wonderful children who filled her loving heart with joy, life was often a struggle. Chessie lived in one of the world's most color-conscious nations. From conception to the grave being black meant oppression.

Coping with little money and lean opportunities had always been a way of life for Chessie. And though the pain was always acute, Chessie's keen intellect and Christian heart helped to keep her from bitterness in the face of frequent brushes with bigotry. Although she accepted the reality of racism and poverty, she felt a tremendous burden for the children she saw in the inner city and outlying areas, and knew their "reality" just had to change.

Days passed before Chessie took another one of her "thinking drives." These getaways allowed relief from the confining cafeteria duties. Since her last trip into town, Chessie seemed haunted by the plight of the children she'd seen.

One morning after breakfast, she managed to pull herself away from her duties at the college and take a drive into the city. Chessie hoped that on this trip, just maybe she would not see what she'd seen before. Driving slowly, she glanced out the left window of her car and soon noticed three young children—two boys and a little girl—each struggling with an armful of pop bottles.

Stopping her car, she leaned out and cheerfully asked, "Where are you going this morning?"

"We goin' to the store," one of the boys answered.

"I see you've got a lot of pop bottles," Chessie commented.

"Yes'm we found 'em and we gonna get some money to buy 'tata chips and candy," the boy continued.

"Did you have any breakfast this morning?" Chessie asked, as her eyes moved searchingly over the scraggly children.

"No ma'am, we ain't had no breakfast," the other boy replied.

With apprehension etched on her face, Chessie questioned further. "Where's your mama and daddy? Who's at home taking care of you?"

Glancing at each other and then looking downward, the little boy replied, "Me and him (pointing to the smaller boy) ain't got no daddy. Mama didn't come home last night, and we don't know where she's at."

"My daddy is sleepin' on the couch," the little girl quickly volunteered. "He would hit me if I woke him up," she blurted, then began to cry.

By this time Chessie had left the car and hurried to the child's side.

"It's all right, Precious. Just let it out. Now tell me all about it." As Chessie knelt to wipe the girl's tears, the sobbing youngster told a sad story. "Daddy and his girlfriend had a big fight last night. She moved out 'cause she didn't want to take care of me and my cousins. Then daddy got drunk and is still on the couch." As the story unfolded, Chessie also learned that during the fight, the girlfriend called her daddy and the children awful names and said she would never be back.

Chessie's heart ached. "Must the children always suffer?" she thought. "Don't they deserve to be considered *first* some of the time?"

Suddenly, Chessie had an idea. "If the parents don't take care of their responsibility, then I will do what I can," she thought.

"Meet me right here, at the same time—on the same corner—tomorrow morning," she said emphatically, making sure the children understood. "I'll bring you something to eat. How about that?"

Grinning widely, the three youngsters promised they'd meet her the next day and, after shifting their load of bottles, continued on their way to the store. Returning to her car, Chessie watched the enterprising little ones turn the corner and disappear. She paused for a moment, clutching her warm jacket to her breast. It would be an eternity before the scene of small children scuffling along in the chilly November air with ashen legs and no socks left her mind.

The next morning Chessie returned to the corner just as she had promised. Sure enough, sitting on the curb were the two small boys and the frail-looking girl. What a pitiful sight! Three children shivering in the cold, each with runny noses, and wearing nothing warmer than short-sleeved, dirty T-shirts.

Managing a cheerful smile, Chessie parked the car and asked the children to hop in. She proceeded to open a bag containing biscuits, grits, scrambled eggs, and small cartons of milk. Their individual paper plates and plastic forks in hand, the children literally devoured the food.

As she watched the children shovel the food into their mouths, Chessie knew that their hunger was as much emotional as physical, and they craved the love she gave them as much as they did the food.

With their tummies full, the children finally stopped eating. Chessie wrapped the remaining biscuits in napkins and each child had a small bundle to take with him. She left that day with a wonderful exhilaration pounding in her heart.

The weeks passed quickly. As Chessie brought food to these children on a regular basis, it occurred to her that there must be others. She began to cruise in different neighborhoods. She found more hungry children and included them in her meal stops.

One morning she spotted four children begging in front of a dime store. Parking her car so as not to be noticed, she watched the children, who appeared to be between eight and eleven years old, stretch out their hands to strangers and appeal for money. The tattered children seemed to annoy passers-by who were nearly stumbling over them in their hurry to move past them and do their shopping.

Chessie's mother-heart ached as she recognized the desperation of the children's situation. The pleas for money were turned down again and again. Occasionally, some generous soul placed a dime or quarter into the little outstretched hands, and the children rejoiced over such a gift.

Chessie watched intently as one passer-by, a well-dressed man, paused momentarily only to snarl, "Get the hell out of my way!"

Chessie flinched when she heard the words. She watched the faces of the children as their hopes disintegrated, crashing on the rocks of reality. Poverty was stealing their childhood.

Unable to stand it any longer, Chessie left the car and approached the children.

"People haven't been very nice to you, have they?" she asked, as she gathered them around her.

"No ma'am," one boy volunteered. He pointed to the car pulling out of the parking lot. "That man cussed us. We only got a dollar so far, and we got to split it four ways."

"There's not much you can buy with a quarter, is there?" Chessie said, shaking her head from side to side.

"No, ma'am. It ain't much, but it will buy us some candy 'cause we's all hungry."

Chessie told these children where to meet her so they could be included in her meal stops. Including these four children, now there would be twenty to feed daily. But she didn't mind. They were hungry.

Heading back home that day after completing her round of meal stops, Chessie felt led to drive an unfamiliar route. The street ended near a poultry house where chickens were killed and packaged for the markets in town. She noticed a rumpled-looking boy about thirteen years old standing near a discard barrel. An attendant dumped unusable chickens (unusable because they had gone bad or were diseased) into the barrel by the shovelfuls. She parked her car and watched from a distance, curious as to what the boy would do.

The youngster ran to the barrel and grabbed a chicken each time the attendant went back into the building. By the time the attendant returned the boy had disappeared behind some large bushes near the side of the building. Watching intently, Chessie finally saw the boy running through the alley and down a parallel street, clutching a tin bucket.

"I must find out where he's going," she said, her curiosity getting the best of her. She followed the lad for three blocks before he darted into a dilapidated shack. Getting out of her car and stepping around the trash, clutter, and debris, she went to the door and knocked. The boy, with dull-looking eyes, opened the door and stared—his mouth slightly agape. "May I come in?" Chessie asked courteously. The boy nodded and gestured toward an old woman stirring a pot of hot water on top of a potbellied stove.

Glancing around, Chessie was stunned by the filth. She

sucked in her breath to avoid the putrid stench that permeated the one-room shack.

"My name is Chessie Harris." Chessie smiled pleasantly at the boy and the old woman who was apparently his grandmother.

"Pleased to meet you. I'm Mattie Barker," the old woman said. "This here is my grandson, Jimmy."

Feeling a little awkward, Chessie told the grandmother of seeing the boy grab the chickens and how she followed him home. Responding with emptiness in her voice, the grandmother said, "That's 'bout all we get to eat. I tries to make it on my little pension, but we ain't never got enough to buy food and pay the utility bills too." Despair was in her voice.

"Jimmy's my daughter's boy." The woman's eyes seemed to lighten just a bit as she looked at her grandson. "His mama went to Chicago three years ago to find work. I ain't heard from her since. Looks like she done forgot about us."

Jimmy stood motionless by the door, his dull eyes watching as his ears listened to every word.

"He's slow," grandmother spoke again. "He can't keep up in school, and he ain't got no decent clothes. So he don't go to school. But he's a big help to me. Gets them chickens for me as often as he can."

Chessie moved slowly toward the woman. "I can see you need help, and I'm going to see what I can do. Just hang on," she said.

With a heavy heart Chessie returned home. What could she do to help this boy and his grandmother? Where should she go? To whom could she turn for help? Suddenly, she thought of her church. Surely the Welfare Organization of the Oakwood College Church could be helpful.

After making a few phone calls, Chessie returned to Mrs. Barker and Jimmy with a carload of clothes and staple food items. They were so grateful that Chessie felt she would burst with joy. Deep inside her soul, however, she knew this was just a temporary solution that could meet only their immediate needs. In a few months their situation would be the same again. Once again, her thoughts turned to all the children she now fed regularly.

Chessie replayed the scenario in her mind over and over—that of black men, unable to find work, hustling to make it the best way they could. And the mothers who worked as maids, cooks, and housekeepers, barely making enough to survive.

Then there were the parents who deserted their children, unable to cope with their responsibilities. Once gone, the parents just seemed to forget about the unwanted youngsters. And if the authorities were fortunate enough to track down any relatives, they would often point out their own desperate circumstances and refuse to take the children in. This constant struggle for survival often drove the neglected children to beg and steal their way through each discouraging day.

"Lord, show me what I can do to help these children, and I will follow your lead," Chessie prayed. The burden she felt for the neglected little ones of Alabama seemed to expand with each passing day. She remembered the poor children she'd seen as a child and often pondered the scenes of oppression endured by her people. All the appalling drama of days gone by, as told to her by her deceased grandmother, Caroline Ray, crowded to the front of her consciousness. She recalled her own poverty-stricken childhood—living as a black sharecropper's daughter, with little hope for the future. And as if in a time tunnel, Chessie's memory took her on a painful journey into the past.

Chapter 2

What About Tomorrow?

Is not this the fast that I have chosen? to loose the hands of wickedness, to undo the heavy burdens, and to let the oppressed go free, and that ye break every yoke? Is it not to deal thy bread to the hungry, and that thou bring the poor that are cast out to thy house? when thou seest the naked, that thou cover him; and that thou hide not thyself from thine own flesh? (Isaiah 58:6, 7).

"Why do we have to live in 'Little Texas?' " thought the chubby eight-year-old girl with snapping black eyes and ebony skin. She stood on the wooden porch of her family's tin-roofed shanty, staring at the endless rows of cultivated clay just beyond the borders of the neatly raked dirt yard.

She knew that wealthy whites in Macon County, Alabama, owned most of the land for hundreds of miles in all directions. But in "Little Texas," "shotgun" houses dotted the countryside. The vestiges of slavery loomed everywhere as straw-hatted Negroes eeked out a meager existence in the fields of massive plantations.

To Chessie, their isolated community was next to nowhere. And Tuskegee, a mere eleven miles away, seemed as far as Memphis or Atlanta.

Sometimes she was allowed to accompany her papa, John Thomas ("Tom") Walker, to town. Tom, whose light-brown skin was tanned by the sun, tried his best to shield his two daughters from the pain of prejudice.

On one of the trips to Tuskegee in her father's buggy, Chessie eagerly soaked up all the sights and sounds of the surrounding countryside.

"Who owns all that land over there, Papa?" she asked.

"Oh, that belongs to Mr. Crenshaw. He owns most of the property in this county," Papa replied.

"He must be rich," Chessie commented.

"Oh, yeah. He's rich all right. He owns several stores in town and has a big dairy farm that supplies milk to folks living as far as a hundred miles away." Papa spoke with a rare longing in his voice.

As the pair reached the outskirts of town she exclaimed, "Papa, these are the biggest, prettiest houses I have ever seen."

Mansions with expansive verandas, and perfectly manicured lawns stood stately back from the streets. She noticed beautifully coiffured white women move gracefully in flowing dresses while carefree children frolicked on lush, green grass. The opulence and beauty awed her.

"Now, see that house right there?" Papa pointed to the mansion on the left. "That's Mr. Crenshaw's."

The two-and-a-half story red-brick structure with a circular, graveled driveway was the most beautiful of all. Chessie's attention quickly moved from the house to the children playing on the front lawn. They were so dressed up to be playing outside. Frilly dresses on the girls and crisp, short pants on the boys looked out of place for playtime. But it soon became clear when the black servants moved a table from the veranda outside that somebody was having a birthday party. Maids in black and white uniforms began to pour punch as the children rushed for a refreshing drink.

"I wish I could have a birthday party like that," Chessie thought to herself.

Papa pulled the horse and buggy to the hitching post. Chessie jumped down, clutching a prized nickel in her little fist. She skipped lightly toward the ice cream parlor in the drug store. She'd been anticipating the new taste sensation of ice cream for several weeks.

Meanwhile, Tom Walker joined a group of fellow sharecroppers standing near the general store. All listened intently as Preacher Saul Jackson described the status of the dying plantation system.

"Whites run plantations for profit, and yet we ain't gettin' our share," Preacher Saul grumbled. "We break our backs all season, only to be told there ain't no money left to pay us. We's so deep in debt to the boss man, we can't even feed and clothe our young'uns. I hear folks is leavin' the South in droves lookin' for work and a better life up north. The white folks is worried, y'all. They don't know how they are gonna make it without us." Heads nodded in agreement.

Tom, whose opinions were respected because he was literate and a deacon in the church, felt compelled to speak up.

"They ought to be worried," Tom began, feeling a burning rage boil up within. "Our babies are starving. Our children ain't got decent clothes. We ain't gettin' paid our fair and rightful share for turning a good crop. We can't make it from one payoff to the next without borrowing from the white man. You know the Bible says, 'Thou shalt not steal.' The boss man been stealing our share of the crop and keeping us down for so long, we gonna have to figure out a way to get out. Leaving the South is probably our best bet."

With those words, Tom proceeded inside the general store. By this time Chessie arrived at the drug store. She burst through the front door with a light heart. Her mouth watered at the sight of sugar cones piled high with the icy delight.

"I would like an ice cream cone, please," Chessie said politely to the man behind the counter, then hesitated when she saw his face. A dark shadow creased his brow and lingered like a cloudy day.

"I'll serve you this time," the man said. "But the next time you come in, use the back door—nigger gal."

Chessie's head snapped back sharply as the words pierced her heart. This was her first brush with bigotry. Looking him straight in the eye as she took the cone, she responded, "Yes, sir." There was pain on her face and contempt on his.

Later, as Chessie and her father rode home, she told him

what happened. "I'm sorry. I should have told you to use the back entrance to the store," he sighed.

"But, Papa," Chessie innocently asked, "why should we have to use the back door anyway?"

"China Doll," he affectionately called her, "there are some things like Jim Crow that are hard to explain. The two races, black and white, have been segregated by law for a long time. We's treated different from white folks just because of the color of our skin. It ain't right, but that's how it is, and we just have to accept it. Just keep on livin' and you'll see what I mean."

"Jim Crow. Segregation," Chessie thought as they rode home. "I don't like segregation now and I know I never will."

From that day on, Chessie's level of awareness and curiosity about her status in life intensified. She began to see and experience the contrast between the white people in town and her life in "Little Texas." The people living near her existed in dilapidated shanties with worn furnishings, and there was an absence of laughter—little to make the black children happy.

Going to church once a week, however, did provide a break in the depressing sharecropper's routine. John Thomas and Lilly Belle Walker, Chessie's parents, took Chessie and her younger sister, Gertrude, to church. Riding in their horse-drawn buggy, they always passed families who couldn't afford to ride, but walked to the Sunday services. Chessie took special notice of the children trudging along beside their parents. Most did not have "dress-up" clothes for church like she did. Many wore the same shoes to school. Some had on dresses and pants much too long or too short. She noticed their sad eyes and frail frames and couldn't help but think that they probably wouldn't have much to eat for Sunday dinner because most of them didn't have more than a biscuit or cold baked potato to bring for their lunch on school days.

Then Chessie would glance down at her own shiny black Mary Jane slippers and white socks and almost wish she didn't have them.

"Why can't all children be happy?" she thought. "Why should they have to suffer?"

But that's the way things were in Macon County, and in

many other places during the years before World War I.

Independent and pensive, Chessie enjoyed spending time alone. One summer afternoon when she was still eight years old, she walked across an open cornfield on the way to visit her grandmother, who lived just on the other side of it. She was thinking about the children she saw on other Macon County farms, the ones who never seemed to smile, the ones who never looked like the pictures she saw in books. Recalling the reality of life in "Little Texas," she fell into a momentary depression.

What about tomorrow? What assurance did she have of a better future?

As Chessie walked through the field, the cornstalks seemed to hear and understand her dilemma. She lifted her heart to God as she had been taught to do by her grandmother whenever she needed help. She felt His presence from above and spoke out loud to Him. As she lifted her eyes to the sky, she tearfully vowed, "Oh, Lord, if you'll let me live to be grown and get an education, I'll do somethin' to make children happy. I'll feed them, clothe them, and let them know I care."

Finishing her prayer of commitment, Chessie discovered she'd picked a full ear of corn. Holding it tightly she marveled at the beauty of the plump yellow kernels.

"I want to see children full and beautiful," she said to herself, as she continued on to her grandmother's. By the time she reached the little shanty her eyes were dry and "mama" didn't suspect that Chessie was sad.

But Chessie didn't forget the vow she'd made. From the depths of her subconscious a desire lay quivering that one day, she would help children be happy. She didn't know how, but she knew she would. And inside her heart she felt the faint stirrings of a future work to be done.

Spring came early that year. Violets peeked through rust-colored soil. Daffodiled front yards and bursting redbuds brightened the fading spirits of sharecroppers in "Little Texas." But uncertainty hung in the air as thick as the smell of the long-needled pines.

Life in this depressed community east of Tuskegee became an ever increasing struggle for survival. Chessie's parents had settled not far from where their parents had been plantation slaves, and sharecropping was all they (Chessie's grandparents) knew. But Chessie's papa wanted his daughters to go to college someday. He inspired intellectual pursuits to free them from the mire of poverty. He had attended Tuskegee Institute and was active with the county's black school system. Tom read constantly, and there were always scads of books and papers lying around the home.

Because of her family's encouragement, Chessie entered Tuskegee in 1918 and two years later Gertrude enrolled.

Soon after this—tired of working his fingers to the bone with nothing to show for it and knowing he must make more money if his kids were to remain in school—Tom Walker made a decision.

"We're movin' to Cleveland," he announced to Lilly Belle one night at supper. He had decided to move north to find one of the industrial jobs that had begun attracting millions of southern blacks during the war.

Jobs—dirty, low-paying, but regular—were available in thriving urban industries to anyone with a mind to work and a back strong enough for heavy lifting.

About six months after the Walkers moved to Cleveland, they wrote the girls that it was time for them also to leave. Gertrude left, but Chessie stayed behind because she had found a full-time job and could attend school in the evenings. After another year passed, however, the money ran out, and she, too, had to leave school.

Papa sent her money for a train ticket, and sadly she packed her belongings. Clearly a girl from the backwoods, she boarded the train one night, carrying her suitcase tied with a piece of rope.

As the train sped toward the north, she began to cry. Her sobbing increased and continued throughout the trip.

"How will I ever be able to help children if I don't finish my education?" Chessie bemoaned her fate as the familiar landscape of her beloved Alabama flashed fleetingly by.

Chapter 3
Ohio's Children

Fear thou not; for I am with thee: be not dismayed; for I am thy God: I will strengthen thee; yea, I will help thee; yea, I will uphold thee with the right hand of my righteousness (Isaiah 41:10).

"Please, Lord, make a way for me to get back to Alabama!" Chessie prayed daily, as the filthy streets of Cleveland's concrete ghettos drove her to depression. Strangely, she also felt overwhelmed with guilt. Her feelings were so strong for the neglected poor of her home state, that she felt she was morally obligated to return. She felt like she had left them alone— alone in the world to be destroyed.

The hoped-for prosperity of the Roaring Twenties never materialized for the Walker family. Tom took whatever jobs he could find while Chessie's mother went to work as a "domestic." Chessie became a doctor's receptionist and tried to finish her high-school degree at night school. Times were tough, and the years sped silently on.

Gradually, Chessie adjusted to city life, but she hated Ohio! As the determined girl settled into a routine of work, work, work, and more work, she soon became aware there were also deprived children in Cleveland. Her heart ached when walking through the inner city. She saw the narrow concrete streets—rutted and filthy—that served the black community. Houses were dismal and small. From time to time little black faces often peered out of upper-story tenement house windows.

"How can they stand the heat?" she thought to herself one summer day when the temperature soared over 95°F. The dirty yards, the flies buzzing in and out of torn window screens, the entire inner city scene projected a sense of things breaking down—of rot and decay.

"What can I do to help the children living in these conditions?" Chessie wondered. She turned the dilemma over and over in her mind.

The big city with its polluted environment, hustle for survival, and lack of trees and fresh air made life once again seem very sad. Chessie longed for the open space and country-fresh atmosphere of Alabama. And in her heart she felt a burning desire to do something now to help the destitute black children living in Cleveland.

Soon it became apparent to Chessie that she could help the children living near her by persuading her parents to take in foster kids. So the family became licensed and started caring for homeless and neglected girls.

As Chessie lavished love upon the little ones placed within her care, she felt a slight easing of the overwhelming burden she carried for destitute children. Yet, within her heart she remembered the children living in "Little Texas" and vowed that someday, somehow, she would return to Alabama and make good on her promise to make them smile.

This dream helped her complete her high-school education, and in the spring of 1923, she graduated. Soon life took on a new glow. She was finding success at her job and beginning to socialize.

One day in 1931, quite by accident, she met a young man named George Harris. He was outside her apartment waiting for a ride to work one morning, when Chessie came outside and they were introduced.

"He has such a nice chuckle," Chessie kept thinking to herself. "He really seems happy—that's the type of person I'd like to be around."

It wasn't long until they began dating. George, a southerner, too, was born in Memphis, grew up in Arkansas, and served in the army during the war. Afterward like Chessie, he moved north with his family. They continued dating for two years, and then in 1933 drove across the state line to Sharon, Pennsylvania, and were married by a justice of the peace.

"Now I won't have to beat back the stresses of life alone," she thought.

Her new husband radiated kindness and love. Chessie soon recognized that here was someone who could help her fulfill her promise to care for children. George, an only child, knew what it meant to be poor and mistreated.

Soon the daughter and son of sharecroppers worked themselves into a comfortable middle-class neighborhood near stores and good schools. Chessie started a catering business, then obtained a real estate license. George did well on his job for a Cleveland galvanizing company, and after their first child*—George—was born, they bought a house in a Cleveland suburb. In spite of this, Chessie still longed to raise her family far from the vice of city life, and in a place large enough to accommodate foster children.

"Honey, why don't we pray and ask God to help us get a farm?" George suggested one day.

The couple began to lean heavily on God's promises as they sought His direction in this desire. Each night they prayed, "Lord, we know that if we trust You and commit our ways to You, You will give us the desires of our hearts."

To their delight and amazement, Chessie and George watched God answer their prayers. Before long, they sold their little house and bought a 105-acre farm an hour's drive from Cleveland. The Lord's timing couldn't have been better because they had added three other children—Chester, Marilyn and Joan (who were still small)—to their family.

---

*George Jr. was the first child of Chessie and George's marriage. However, at this time, there were two children from previous marriages. Herbert, Chessie's son, and Bernice (now deceased), George's daughter. The four children mentioned in this story are Chessie and George's.

"Now, I can bring lots of children out to the farm from the city," Chessie told her family. North Elim Farm was a little bit of heaven on earth. A perfect place for children. The beige, two-story, five-bedroom house had a full basement and spacious rooms. There were a sturdy barn, smoke house, and acres of sloping land surrounded by a forest of towering trees. The natural beauty of the land, the many birds and wild animals made it a delightful place to live. Soon they began inviting youngsters from the city for visits and picnics.

"Lord, I feel like I've come home," Chessie prayed with a thankful heart as she ministered to the children of that area. They came scared and abused, ragged, dirty, shoeless, their faces full of ache and suffering, privation, hunger, and lost human dignity. But after being with the Harris family for a little while, the children became more secure and would smile and laugh, which made Chessie's heart sing with joy.

Some of the children had never seen farm animals, and Chessie and George were determined to teach them about nature and expose them to the natural beauties of life. In the warmer months the back slopes of the farm became a picnic ground—a place to sing, pray, and learn of God. Chessie determined in her heart that each child under her influence would learn of the Creator of the universe and His bountiful blessings.

Those times it snowed they would hitch a team of horses to the sleigh that George had made and spend many happy hours sliding over the crusty ice. Shouts of glee rang clear in the frosty air. Warm breath formed airy clouds of white in the cold air as horses pulled the happy group swiftly over the back slopes of North Elim Farm. "Thank You, Lord, for nature's inexpensive pleasures," Chessie would pray as she praised God for His many blessings.

But learning about life was more than fun and games. "Children must learn how to work," George said. George spent a great deal of time teaching the youngsters how to milk cows, bale hay, prune trees, make maple syrup, and hunt in the woods. Chessie was thrilled to see these children receiving the loving attention and training that would make them responsible citizens one day. She loved her work, but she nevertheless felt the enormity of the task. Many nights after George was asleep, Chessie would slip out of bed long before daylight and talk with God. "Give me guidance and wisdom in raising all the children you've placed in my care, heavenly Father. And continue blessing so we can provide for these dear little ones."

Then as a postscript to her prayers, Chessie would remind God of the promises she'd made in the cornfield—of her concern for the little Alabama children who didn't enjoy even the basics of life—let alone any simple pleasures.

Rising from her knees, Chessie would slide back into bed beside George. After pondering her prayer for a few moments, she'd feel peace. She knew that in God's own time He would answer according to His will. He always had before. "Perhaps God has a work for me to do here in Ohio," she thought, and for the moment, pushed thoughts of returning to Alabama out of her mind.

Chapter 4

Call to Alabama

Ask, and it shall be given you; seek, and ye shall find; knock, and it shall be opened unto you: for every one that asketh receiveth; and he that seeketh findeth; and to him that knocketh it shall be opened. Or what man is there of you, whom if his son ask bread, will he give him a stone? (Matthew 7:7-9).

———————————

The winter of 1949 finally gave way to spring. On North Elim Farm the apple orchard projected a bumper crop. The soybeans were in, and blades of green poked through the rich brown soil. It looked like a promising year.

One Saturday morning Chessie, George, and their brood sat in the Cleveland church they regularly attended. As she thought about their four children, in a nearly all-white school, Chessie was especially concerned about fourteen-year-old George, Jr. ("Bo"). He was good looking, charismatic, and an outstanding athlete. The girls swooned over him.

Just the previous week, a farmer in the area threatened to harm the boy if he ever caught him with his daughter again. What the farmer didn't know was that his sixteen-year-old daughter was actually chasing her son—rather than the reverse. And besides, interest in girls was to be expected at this age. The problem was, there weren't any black girls in the area. What was Bo to do? How were they ever going to handle this potentially explosive situation?

As the guest speaker for the church service described a

Christian boarding academy in Alabama, Chessie and George listened intently. The recruitment speech convinced them that Bo should attend this academy. It would provide the kind of Christian environment they wanted for all of their children. But most important, it offered opportunities for Bo to relate to other black young people in an academic setting.

After some investigation, the Harrises enrolled Bo in Oakwood Academy in Huntsville, Alabama.

As Bo struggled throughout the year, Chessie and George, far away from him, prayed continually and wrote letters of encouragement. They gave him pep talks when he came home for holidays.

"You've got to keep your mind on your studies, Son, and not on the girls," George charged.

Bo found himself the target of admiration by many girls. His social life now flourished! Yet, the teachers had told him if his grades didn't improve, he couldn't remain in school.

When their son came home for the summer, Chessie and George could see that he really did want to make a success of his school opportunities. And yet they felt that he would do much better if he could be at home. But what were they to do? They prayed earnestly, asking for God's guidance.

Then one sunny July morning in 1950 the phone rang.

"Mrs. Harris?" a deep voice inquired. "This is Paul Ashford from Oakwood College in Huntsville, Alabama."

"Why, yes, Mr. Ashford, I'm surprised to hear from the college," Chessie responded, knowing that Bo was still in high school. "What can I do for you?"

"Mrs. Harris," he continued rather hesitantly, "we're in dire need of a food service director for our college cafeteria and a grounds superintendent and farm manager. You and your husband seem to have special abilities in these areas. We feel that as a couple you could meet our needs. We've heard about you from some of your son's teachers. Would you consider moving to Alabama and working at the college?"

Would she! Chessie felt as if she'd been struck by a bolt of lightning. She sat down on the wooden chair by the phone.

"I can't believe it, Mr. Ashford! You want George and me to

come down and work for the college?"

"Yes, Mrs. Harris. We know your son has been here in school and thought it would be a good move for your family. We will take care of your moving expenses and find temporary housing for you until you find a place of your own," Mr. Ashford replied.

Still stunned with disbelief, Chessie shouted for joy after she hung up the phone. "Thank You, Jesus," she said as she ran out the door toward the barn where George was working. Here was the answer to her long-standing prayer.

"Thank You, Lord, thank You! I asked You to let me get back to Alabama, but you didn't tell me it would be this way," she whispered.

That evening when the family gathered for worship, Chessie selected special songs and Bible verses for each child to read. She had something very important to discuss.

"I want all of you to listen very closely to what I am going to say," she began.

"I've been praying about something for many years. And today, the Lord has answered my prayer!"

She reviewed the story of the promise she made to God when she was a little girl and described the needs of children in the South. She told her family about the phone call from Mr. Ashford and how she saw this as the answer to her prayers.

The family sank to their knees and George (Papa) offered the closing prayer. "Lord," he began, "we thank You for fixing it so that we have a way to serve You better. We have leaned on You through the years. You have guided and directed our every step. And now, Lord, show us what You want us to do and how You want us to do it."

After worship everybody started talking at once. Who would be going? How would they get there? What would it be like in Alabama? Chessie didn't have answers to all the questions. But foremost in her mind was what they would do with the six foster children living with them.

That night she and George talked together. "I love the farm and the success it's become," George said quietly. "I'm making good on my job here in Cleveland with more than twenty years seniority. We have sufficient funds, ample food, many children to care for, and have all we've ever dreamed of in Ohio." He paused for a moment, then continued, "But if you see light in it, Honey, we will go."

This affirmation sent chills of joy racing through Chessie's body. She wanted so much for George to be as excited as she felt inside. He was not. But for now, just his approval was enough.

Chessie's mind went into high gear. She managed most of the business affairs of the household. Many details had to be worked out. The farm must be sold or rented as well as the animals and equipment. Whatever crops were ready must be harvested so they wouldn't lose all of their investment in that year's planting. So much to be done—so little time before the beginning of the school year. Chessie knew that God was equal to the tasks ahead.

Two o'clock in the morning rolled around. Chessie slipped out of bed for her time with the Lord.

"If you want us to go, Lord, You work it out. You have our willing hands and hearts. I trust in Your promises and praise Your name for answering my prayer. If it is Your will that we go, let everything be sold by the time we come back from the market tomorrow afternoon."

The family arose early as usual. Chessie and the boys took the farm produce and went to market. George and the girls remained behind. When Chessie and the children returned to the farm about two o'clock that afternoon, *all the farm equipment was gone!* George stood in the door waiting to give her the news.

"What happened? Everything is gone!" Chessie said, throwing her arms around her somewhat dazed husband.

"We sold everything. I mean everything!" George answered. "Folks came from all over and bought *everything.*"

"That's it!" Chessie cried. "Now I know without a doubt that the Lord wants us back in Alabama. Let's pack."

Chessie couldn't quite believe they were actually going until the movers drove their truck out of the long gravel driveway of

North Elim Farm. Though they were leaving it behind, the farm itself was still theirs for the moment. They decided it was best to rent it out until a buyer could be found.

By this time, most of the foster children had returned to live with other families in the area. But two of the older boys, Claude* and Toney,* begged and cried to go with the Harris family. The authorities finally gave permission for them to leave the state with the Harrises.

A few weeks later, loaded up in the Buick, the family waved their last goodbyes to the farm as they departed for the long journey to Alabama. George, Chessie, their four children, along with Claude and Toney, were anxious for their new life in Alabama. As they traveled along on that sunny August day, they sang songs and listened as George and Chessie told of their experiences in the South.

As the car rolled on mile after mile, Chessie's mind recalled many of her childhood days. The sad faces of the farm children seemed to flash on the screen of her consciousness.

"At long last we're on our way home," she sighed.

But little could she know of the trials and heartaches ahead.

---

*All names of foster children mentioned throughout this book have been changed to protect their privacy.

Chapter 5

Shadows

God is our refuge and strength, a very present help in trouble. Therefore will not we fear, though the earth be removed, and though the mountains be carried into the midst of the sea; though the waters thereof roar and be troubled, though the mountains shake with the swelling thereof. Selah (Psalm 46:1-3).

———————————

The first heartache the Harris family experienced was not being able to find a place to live.

"There just doesn't seem to be an affordable house anywhere large enough to house a family of eight," Chessie sighed, as she and the two girls lugged suitcases and boxes up a flight of stairs in the girls' dormitory of Oakwood College. With nowhere else to stay, she and the girls decided to move into the women's residence hall, and George and the boys took two rooms in the boy's dormitory.

They expected to be there only a few days, but it turned out to be the arrangement for several months. Living apart with all of their earthly possessions scattered made it difficult to maintain the sense of family unity and security they all needed.

"We'll do the best we can, work hard, and continue praying for a house," Chessie encouraged George and the children daily. Finding a way for the family to be together again became a burning desire.

Meanwhile, Chessie began her job in the college cafeteria,

and George started his work taking care of the campus grounds.

In the fall of 1950, a small house located at the foot of a hill became available for rent. It was surrounded by maples, huge oaks, and various kinds of evergreens. The location was perfect, but it had only two bedrooms, living room, dining area, kitchen, and bath.

"It will do just fine, and the price is reasonable," Chessie decided immediately after inspecting it thoroughly.

She realized that what was most important was for the family to be together. The next week they moved in. They made the best of what they had by the boys sharing one room with two sets of bunk beds. Then the girls crowded into the other bedroom while Chessie and George sectioned off a portion of the living room for their bedroom. Happy to be together, no one complained.

The months flew by. George enjoyed his work on campus. He took pride in showing the student workers what needed to be done and how to do it. He supervised planting and harvesting. In addition, the campus grounds were manifestations of his handiwork—well-manicured lawns, lush flowering shrubs, and neatly trimmed hedges. George definitely had a green thumb, and his knowledge of plants and flowers made this a job he thoroughly enjoyed.

Chessie also did an outstanding job with her responsibilities as Director of the Cafeteria and Food Service.

Once again life took on a glow. Bo improved scholastically in the academy. Chester, Marilyn, and Joan adjusted beautifully at the campus elementary school. The only shadow in their lives now was the realization that Claude and Toney would have to return to Ohio. They just could not adjust to life in Alabama. Everyone felt sad about this arrangement, but it was best for everyone.

Life now seemed secure, in spite of financial limitations. Chessie and George weren't making nearly the amount of money they had been accustomed to in Ohio. Yet they had enough to get by and reason to be thankful. Still, in spite of Chessie's pleasant exterior, and the fact that she was working hard taking care of 300 to 400 young people on the college campus, her heart was nearly breaking as she observed the poor children in and around Huntsville.

One evening her discontent surfaced, and Chessie confided in her husband, "Honey, these young people here at the college really don't need me—not like the children I see every day in the city."

As she rode around town on various errands, she saw the poor housing sections near downtown. She observed kids poking through trash bins at supermarkets and stealing food from the loading docks.

"Those are the children who really need me," she said to George.

He sat quietly for a moment and then said, "Well, what do you want to do about it?"

Chessie didn't quite know what she wanted to do about her restlessness. And that's when she began taking her "thinking drives" around the Huntsville area. The deplorable situations she encountered as she cruised the back alleys in town and the dirt country roads of the rural poor haunted her constantly. Steadily, the seriousness of what being black and deprived meant to the children she saw day after day fanned a spark of social sensitivity.

"These ARE the children I'm to help!" The thought crystallized in her mind. Furthermore she recognized that these children were learning firsthand that being poor brings pain— that the color of one's skin often brings oppression—especially in America, one of the world's most color-conscious nations.

"I must do something to help them." Always in an attitude of prayer, Chessie petitioned her heavenly Father. "Lord, show me what to do, and I will follow your lead."

The winter months of 1951 were nearly over. Mild days and chilly nights invigorated the Harris family as they carried on their daily routine. Chessie continued her downtown and countryside trips, and her "think drives" became searches for needy children.

One morning as she drove along a country road, Chessie began singing, as she frequently did while riding alone. "All things bright and beautiful, all creatures great and small. All things wise and wonderful, the Lord God made them all." Her beautiful soprano voice filled the car with joyful praise and brought God's presence near. Nevertheless, the sounds of a crying child somehow caught her ear and temporarily suspended her singing. Chessie stopped the car and listened. The cries seemed to come from a run-down house to the right of where she had stopped. She turned into the mud driveway, exited the vehicle, and approached the rickety front door. Chessie knocked but when no one answered, she pushed the door open and peered inside.

Sitting in the corner of a nearly bare room were three children. A child not more than six years old supervised a toddler and an infant. "I heard someone crying, and I thought I would find out if there was anything I could do to help," Chessie told the six-year-old.

"Both of them's been crying. I don't know what to do. There's no milk for the baby and I'm makin' a fire to cook some grits," the child replied.

Inspecting the children, Chessie found that the baby was soaking wet and had a terrible cold. The toddler was also coughing and seemed irritable as she rubbed her ears. Obviously, all the children were sick.

"Where's your mama or daddy?" Chessie asked as she began to search for a clean diaper.

"Don't know," said the six-year-old. "And Mama's gone somewhere."

Chessie promptly changed the baby and held the toddler on her lap as she washed her face. Her tender touch must have been soothing because the little girl had stopped whining.

Chessie knew what she had to do. "I'm going to the store to get something to eat," she announced cheerily.

After Chessie returned, she busied herself in the kitchen. Not finding much on the shelves to prepare, she felt glad she'd had some extra money along to buy a few groceries.

After doing all she could, Chessie said goodbye to the children. Her heart ached at the thought of leaving them there, but she comforted herself in the knowledge that their stomachs were full until their mother returned. As she pulled away and headed down the road, she breathed a prayer, "Thank You, Lord, for sending me here at the right time."

Day after day, Chessie continued searching for children, and all the while her frustration was increasing as she encountered more and more desperate situations. Her thoughts would often take her back to her childhood. She remembered and could almost feel the gnawing of an empty stomach. She recalled the embarrassment of wearing tacky clothes, and as she did, the cornfield promise blazed a burning trail in her mind.

For months now Chessie had been feeding the hungry children of Huntsville and taking care of them as best she could. Each day the children, now accustomed to "Mama Harris's" food runs, huddled on city street corners and beside country roads, waiting for her car. Others had been clothed and referred for medical care. Chessie had made a real difference in the lives of these children, but she knew much more needed to be done.

After one of her regular stops, Chessie noticed two little girls lingering nearby. "Run on home now. Your folks will be wondering where you are," Chessie coaxed.

"No they won't, 'cause ain't nobody home," the tallest girl, about nine years old, said.

Chessie took a closer look at the girls and noticed welts and deep scratches on their bodies. She knelt down, lifted the chin of the smaller girl, and asked, "What happened to you? How did you get these?"

"Mama whipped me with a switch," the little girl responded. "She just gets mad like that sometimes."

"Oh Lord," Chessie thought to herself. "Why must they suffer so?"

"You mean you did nothing to deserve the whipping?" Chessie queried.

The older girl chimed in, "We don't have to do somethin' for Mama to get us. People say she is 'mentally.' " Men give her money and she wants us to do somethin' bad with men too. When we don't, we just get beat."

"How could this be?" Chessie thought. "No mother would treat her girls this way!"

Knowing if she went home and left these children in the street she couldn't live with herself, she asked quickly, "Would you like to come home with Mama Harris?"

The girls stared at each other with glee. "Yes'm!" They both spoke at once. With a feeling of joy, Chessie and "her children" piled into the car and headed for home.

When the three of them reached home and went inside, the girls stood nervously inside the front door.

"Come on in," Chessie said. "I want you to meet my family." George, who had just come in from work, spoke in soft tones.

"Hi there." He patted them on the shoulders. "What's your name?" The older girl looked at Chessie, who nodded for her to answer.

"My name is Mamie, and this is my sister, Sadie."

Chessie spoke. "These are our daughters for the day."

"Mighty fine," George answered as he walked down the hallway. "Just make yourselves at home."

Chessie knew their own children would soon be home from music lessons and after-school activities. She quickly led the girls into the bathroom and ran warm water in the tub. She made sure that each of them scrubbed their grimy bodies before shampooing their hair and dressing them in clean clothes.

As she bustled around the homey kitchen, Chessie gave the girls tasks for getting dinner ready. Mamie, the older, grated cheese for the macaroni casserole, while Sadie placed cookie dough on the cookie sheet.

Around 4:30 that afternoon, the four Harris children arrived home from school. They all headed for the kitchen, which was filled with the aroma of oatmeal cookies. Mamie and Sadie at first seemed overwhelmed with all of the loving attention lavished on them. Marilyn and Joan, acting like little mothers, took charge as soon as the girls were finished in the kitchen. Soon, the girls acted as if they'd always been part of the family.

After supper was finished and the dishes were done, the family gathered in the living room for evening worship. Chessie led in singing, "With Jesus in the family, happy, happy, home." She wanted to teach the girls that Jesus can help us have happy homes. They sat snuggled against Chessie, one on each side, as she read the Beatitudes from the Bible.

As the lengthening shadows faded through the front window, Chessie knew she would have to take the children back.

"It's time to take you home now," Chessie said gently. The girls, unwilling to leave their new-found family, began begging, "Mama Harris, can't we spend the night?"

Painfully she responded, "No, Darlings, your folks will be wondering where you are. We must not worry them." Sadie began to cry.

"Now Sadie," Chessie said, holding the little girl close. "God loves you, and when you are afraid just sing this little song: 'Jesus loves me this I know, for the Bible tells me so.'" Sadie knew the song and soon began to sing along with Chessie. Sadie sang all the way home. She felt confident that she could sing it anytime she needed Jesus to be near.

Before the girls got out of the car in the front of their house, Chessie stopped a moment to pray with them.

"Loving Father in heaven, please protect Mamie and Sadie tonight. Amen."

Later, as Chessie lay sleepless next to George, she pondered the fate of the little girls. How would they survive in their jungle of abuse? If this were the only case of neglect or privation she encountered, she could possibly handle it. But she felt convinced now that she wanted to take care of children like Mamie and Sadie. Not for one afternoon, but all the time. She never wanted children like these to return to homes like theirs. But how could she care for more children? Their own family was already crowded in their little house. And although they lived adequately, there wasn't any extra money.

Chessie couldn't read the future, of course. But God, who guides and leads every willing person, had a plan—a plan for her to provide permanent care for the street children of Alabama. What she couldn't know just yet was that the plan would soon unfold, and her dream would become a reality.

Chapter 6

Finding a Legal Way

Blessed is the man that walketh not in the counsel of the ungodly, nor standeth in the way of sinners, nor sitteth in the seat of the scornful. But his delight is in the law of the Lord; and in his law doth he meditate day and night (Psalm 1:1, 2).

———————

The year was 1953. The fading blooms of summer abandoned themselves to autumn's tawny glow.

"We really need a place of our own," Chessie thought one afternoon as she glanced around the rented two-bedroom house the six of them had lived in for the past three years. The lack of privacy, the tiny kitchen, and limited storage space depressed her. She wanted a place where she would have enough room to adequately house some of the needy children she fed daily in Huntsville.

Chessie decided to search in earnest for a different place to live. One afternoon while driving a short distance from the college, she noticed a little house for sale on two acres of land. After inquiring about the price, she went home and approached George about buying the place.

"If you can work it out, Honey, it's OK with me," George said. He seemed perfectly willing to make the financial commitment and change of location.

Within a few weeks the paper work had been completed, the finances taken care of, and the excited family moved in. Again, the house was small, but it had potential for additions or even building a larger structure on the adjoining acre.

By now George Jr. had graduated from high school and was in the army. In order to make room for everyone else, Chessie and George again made the living room their bedroom. Furniture was crammed into every corner. Stumbling over her brown leather couch in the dark one night, Chessie vowed to add on to the house as soon as they could afford it. Although the girls, Marilyn and Joan, had a bedroom of their own and Chester one of his own, Chessie knew they needed at least four bedrooms. The hows and whys of keeping children had thus far been confined to a simple feeding program, and in their present cramped quarters Chessie couldn't envision where they'd put any extras. So she began praying earnestly and meditating. "Lord, You've placed the desire within me to help children, but I need a place to put them. There are so many children that really need me—I must have Your help."

"What I really want to do," she remarked to George one evening, "is provide a permanent home for deprived youngsters—something like an institution. A place with plenty of room, food, and lots of love."

Realistically, though, Chessie was in no position to undertake the enormous task of opening a home for children.

"Show me what to do, Lord," she prayed. "There must be a legal way I can care for children. Please help me find it." Chessie never hesitated to pour out her heart to God, but she did more than praying and waiting idly for a miracle. She set her mind into high gear. Ideas emerged, sparking the birth of a plan. The first thing she decided to do was to contact the local welfare department.

Chessie prayed long and hard before approaching the all-white staff. Never for a moment did she forget that she was black and that the children she cared about most were black. The Jim Crow of years gone by and the segregation of the 1950s was evident everywhere in town. There were still "white" and "colored" benches in the municipal parks, restaurants with take-out service windows cut out for "colored only," because blacks were not allowed inside.

"Will segregation ever be stamped out?" Chessie thought. "Why should children be treated so inhumanely and why should people be treated differently because of the color of their skin?" she questioned within her heart. But the reality of the times made Chessie recognize that she had to be prepared for what she might encounter at the welfare office. Her strong convictions and heartfelt love for "throw-away children," however, left her free to confront any issue that would enable black children to receive the loving care they needed.

On her first visit to the welfare office in Huntsville, Chessie talked with a middle-aged intake worker, Mrs. Foxworthy. She approached the woman with a courteous self-assurance.

"I'm here to talk with you about children who are living in the street," Chessie began. "Children I've seen day after day who have no one to properly care for them. I have been traveling all over the city and in some rural areas of the county and find there are many, many children needing care." Chessie spoke earnestly. "I'm here to offer my services. I'd be glad to help take care of these children—to get them off the streets and out of the shacks they live in, and away from abusive parents and relatives who are neglecting them. I'd like to nurture children, teach them simple skills, and show them I care."

Mrs. Foxworthy, a pert bureaucrat, answered, "Nothing like this has ever been brought to our attention. What children are you talking about?"

Chessie described the areas where she had made frequent meal stops and the rural areas where children were in need.

As the woman listened, Chessie sensed that she was not being believed.

"I'm telling you these things are true," Chessie emphasized.

Mrs. Foxworthy expressed her opinion as flippantly as if the two women weren't even talking about human beings.

"Our child welfare services are more than adequate to investigate and serve children. I'm sure that if there were problems as you describe, our case workers would have brought them to our attention. Perhaps if you provide me with the names and addresses of these needy children you've found, I can assign our caseworkers to talk with the parents."

Chessie sighed. She knew most of the parents of street children remained invisible. The immediate needs of these children demanded action—not talk. Mentally, Chessie had prepared herself for the "who are you—what do you know" attitude she encountered on a regular basis as a black person. She knew she must project a calm confidence and made an instant decision to probe further.

"Surely there must be a place in Madison County where neglected children can be cared for, given something to eat, a bath, or whatever they need," Chessie continued.

"We have no need for that type of care in this county," Mrs. Foxworthy spoke sternly.

What Mrs. Foxworthy did not articulate was that there were no facilities for black children. Chessie knew this was an area of tremendous need, so she asked a leading question.

"What about facilities for white children? Are there homes for them?"

"We do have facilities for white children, but not for colored. We just haven't had a call for them," Mrs. Foxworthy answered matter-of-factly.

"Now the real story is told," Chessie thought to herself.

Deciding to probe further, she asked, "What would happen if these children committed crimes?"

"If there are no relatives to take them, they are placed in the county jail," Mrs. Foxworthy answered.

Aghast, Chessie retorted, "You mean children are put in jail with criminals?"

"Yes. There is no place else for them to go. At least they'd be off the streets."

The woman's cold words raised a storm of resentment within Chessie's breast and surged through her like a bolt of lightning. "How could the system be so cruel to children?" she thought. Then before leaving she said, "Please tell me what is involved in getting a license for more than six children." Certainly that request could easily be handled.

"I'm sorry," Mrs. Foxworthy said. "At this time I'm afraid I can't help you."

Chessie left the welfare office more determined than ever to find a legal way to help needy children. "I'll do it alone if I have to," she thought as she drove home.

That night after family worship, Chessie called a meeting of the Harris family council, which frequently met for the purpose of solving family dilemmas. She reminded her children of their experience in Ohio with foster brothers and sisters. She told them of the children in the Huntsville streets she had seen and how she longed to provide the loving care they needed. She described her visit to the welfare department that day and pledged not to give up in finding a legal way to care for the needy children of Alabama.

"We're going to legally care for deprived children, and somebody somewhere is going to tell us how!" She meant business, and her family understood clearly that when Mama made up her mind to do something, there was no stopping her.

George listened carefully and then spoke with a suppressed twinkle in his eyes. "Well, Babe, you didn't get any answers from that one lady. She's only working for somebody else. Why don't you go to the top?"

Chessie gave her husband a warm hug. She felt so thankful for his support and love. With his encouragement, and with the willingness of her children to accept foster brothers and sisters, she knew she could succeed.

Chessie carefully mapped out her strategy. She did some investigating and contacted a supervisor at the State of Alabama Division of Child Caring Institutions.

Having been given an appointment for the following week, Chessie recognized that she must be thoroughly prepared and businesslike. She went over and over in her mind what she would say and how she might handle any possible skepticism such as she'd experienced with Mrs. Foxworthy of the Huntsville Welfare Department.

"This time I'll inquire about the types of care I can be licensed to provide," she vowed to herself.

The day of her appointment arrived. Dressed neatly in a dress, silk stockings and high heels, she drove the 200 miles to the state capital and was ushered into the office of the child care supervisor, Mrs. Goodson.

Chessie presented her case with eloquent persuasiveness. She described in graphic detail her meal stops and the tremendous deprivation she'd seen. She shared her experience as a foster boarding mother in Ohio and her dream of establishing a home for children in Alabama. Then she asked the crucial question. "What do I need to do to open a child care institution in Alabama?"

Obviously impressed, Mrs. Goodson said, "In our state there are two types of licenses in child care—foster boarding and institutional. There are requirements set down by the state for both. Foster boarding homes are licensed for no more than five children."

"I see," Chessie commented. "Since I want to legally take care of as many children as I can find, I want the child care institution license."

Mrs. Goodson answered, "I can see you are not one to give up easily. My department will give study to your request and get back to you at a later date." Then she continued, "Chessie, in order for anyone to be licensed, someone from our office must do a home study. They will come check out the facilities and determine how many children a home can accommodate. There is also an evaluation as to a person's capability of being a good foster boarding mother."

"This process could take a long time to complete, couldn't it?" questioned Chessie.

"Yes, it could," Mrs. Goodson answered. "Actually, I'd like to suggest that you apply to be a licensed boarding mother in the meantime. This way you'll have legal approval to keep up to five children."

Chessie left the state capital that day feeling she had finally heard some answers. George was right. Going to the top proved helpful. Now she felt anxious to get home and share the news with him and the children.

Later that evening around the dinner table, Chessie told the family the news about her visit with Mrs. Goodson.

"I think I've made progress in getting a license to open a home for children," she said. "And this week I'm going to the local welfare office and apply for a foster boarding license."

Would the welfare department accept her application? She wondered.

Chapter 7

The Children Come

He was oppressed, and he was afflicted, yet he opened not his mouth: he is brought as a lamb to the slaughter, and as a sheep before her shearers is dumb, so he openeth not his mouth (Isaiah 53:7).

Chessie encountered no trouble getting a foster boarding license in June of 1954. And she continued feeding street children. Once or twice each week when her work was done at the Oakwood College cafeteria she loaded as many servings of biscuits, grits, and scrambled eggs as she could carry into her car and posted herself under a tall elm tree on Church Street, looking for the children she'd seen.

She'd stay for an hour or so, feed seven to a dozen children, tell them stories, and try to meet their emotional needs. But always she would come home frustrated because she couldn't do more.

A few weeks after receiving the foster boarding license, a caseworker from the county welfare department called.

"Mrs. Harris, we have an emergency! A baby's been found abandoned. There is nobody to take it. Can you?"

Chessie's thoughts churned quickly. A surge of adrenalin propelled her, and she answered quickly, "Yes, of course! Bring the little one over."

After hanging up the phone, Chessie realized that she had failed to ask any of the important questions. How old was the little one? Was it a boy or girl? Were there any health problems?

44

George was at work when the call came, but Marilyn and Joan jumped for joy when their mother excitedly shared the news with them.

"A baby! I'd hoped we'd take babies all along," Marilyn bubbled.

Within half an hour the young, blond caseworker arrived. She opened the back door of her station wagon, picked up a little bundle, and brought it inside.

Chessie immediately took the child in her arms. Pulling back the cover she looked into the sleeping face of a little girl about six months old.

"We know nothing about this child," the caseworker said. "We just know she was abandoned in a cardboard box in an empty house, and she really needs care."

The circumstances from which the baby came didn't matter to Chessie. She and the girls were so excited that they all began talking at once.

"We'll need clothes, a bed, food, and an appointment at the health department clinic for a physical examination," Chessie told the girls.

"Marilyn, run down to the basement and bring up my mother's old trunk. We'll use that for a bed. Joan, go upstairs and get a feather pillow and an old blanket."

Before long Chessie and the girls had fixed a warm and cozy place for the baby to sleep. While the girls cleaned the baby up, Chessie hurried to the store and bought baby bottles and other needed supplies. Soon the child was fast asleep in her little bed. When George came home that evening they held a family council and decided to name the newest addition to their family "Irene Trunk!"

As the days and weeks passed, Irene was loved and cared for more than any other person in the family.

"She's such a good baby, Mama," Joan said as she rocked the child to sleep one night.

"Yes, she is a good baby, Honey," Chessie answered." And I wish we had an institutional license so we could take in a lot more like her."

A few weeks later the caseworker called again and said,

"Chessie, could you take two little boys about seven and eight years of age? They desperately need a home. It seems their mother died and the father placed them with his aged mother, then left town to work in a distant city. The grandmother is so feeble that the boys are too much for her. Last week she locked them out of the house. They've been eating out of the garbage cans and sleeping in cars near the farmers' market. They need to be off the streets."

"Why of course I'll take the boys. Bring them to me," Chessie said, not knowing where in the world the children would sleep. "We're so crowded," she thought, but she couldn't stand the thought of two vulnerable boys sleeping in abandoned cars and scrounging for throw-away fruits and vegetables!

The next day the caseworker brought the disheveled children to the Harris home. Chessie's heart gave a big lurch when she opened the door and saw the two forlorn children standing—nearly naked—on the steps. They had on what resembled T-shirts, cut off jeans—their little buttocks showing—and no shoes or socks. Their clothes had been slept in, and obviously their hair hadn't been combed for weeks. But the precious boys had clear, bright eyes, and Chessie swept them into her arms and welcomed them home.

Empathy filled the hearts of not only Chessie and George but their children as well. The Harris children seemed to understand the great need of the children coming into their home, and they accepted them as their unofficial brothers and sisters. They welcomed the boys with love and caring attention, willing to share whatever they had with the children.

Now there were six children in the tiny house.

"Where will Bob and Len sleep?" Chessie thought as she bustled around that evening rearranging Chester's room. She had decided to make pallets with quilts on the floor until she could afford another set of bunk beds.

"Come and see the nice bed I've made for you," Chessie lovingly said to the somewhat apprehensive children. One would think these neglected boys would relish sleeping in a nice, clean bed. But oh, no! They shrank back from getting into the pallets with the stark white sheets.

"I don't want to sleep here," Bob, the eldest, whined.

"I think it's too clean, Mama," Joan said wisely. And later Chessie agreed that the white sheets must have somehow reminded the children of death. Sliding down into something so sterile was utterly foreign to the little waifs who had been sleeping outside and in abandoned cars.

"They can have my bed, Mama," Chester spoke up unselfishly. And that night he slept on the floor while the boys took his bed.

The next day Chessie bought some flannel sheets and brightly colored pillowcases. She decided that the children might find these more acceptable. Sure enough, within a few days they settled into the routine and willingly got into their own pallets on the floor.

Chessie noticed that it took the boys about ten days to become accustomed to a new environment. And she patiently bore with the personality traumas the children encountered until they began to feel safe, secure, and loved.

"If we get any more children, we'll absolutely have to have a bigger house," Chessie said to George one evening after the children were in bed.

"But, Honey, we don't have any extra money." He hesitated a minute thinking then continued. "I suppose we could sell North Elim Farm in Ohio instead of renting it out. We'd get a big hunk of money that way."

Chessie looked up in surprise. She knew how much George loved that farm. A warm feeling of love welled up in her breast for her considerate husband. She recalled how just the previous week George had wistfully commented that he'd like to go back and live on the farm. Chessie knew that from George's perspective, life was much easier financially in Ohio.

The idea of selling their Ohio farm badgered Chessie's conscience until she decided to contact a realtor she knew in Cleveland. He agreed to advertise and see what would happen. Before three months had passed, the farm sold.

"I guess the Lord knew we needed the money," George said sorrowfully. "But at least now we have money to build our own house."

It took only a few months to put up the new brick house, and before Christmas, the family of eight were moved and settled. Chessie appreciated having more closet space, but better still she and George could once again have a private bedroom. There was even room now for more children.

To Chessie's amazement, the local caseworker began referring children to the Harris family on a regular basis, apparently ignoring the fact that they were licensed for only five children. Sometimes they had ten or more children staying with them. Three-day-old baby Jay, with his red curly hair, was a favorite. He had come to them wrapped in a raincoat.

Chessie understood very well that the department's growing acceptance of her came about largely because of the dramatic difference the social workers saw in the kids after being at the Harris's house for just a short period.

Children living in the Harris home were given excellent physical and emotional care. Love was lavished on every child, and emotional nurturing was given in spite of the deprivation or mental capacity. The welfare workers recognized that a mother and father in the home overshadowed a high income.

With the growing number of children, Chessie began to recognize that if she were to continue providing quality care, she would need to resign her job at the college.

"I hate to see you give up that income," George said when Chessie confided her conviction about quitting. But he, too, felt that she was needed full time at home.

It was a big decision. But Chessie knew it was the only one she could make and have a clear conscience.

Chapter 8

Roadblocks

The Lord is my light and my salvation; whom shall I fear? the lord is the strength of my life; of whom shall I be afraid? (Psalm 27:1).

———————

One morning after resigning her job, Chessie was sitting on her bed studying her Bible, when suddenly she recalled the conversation she'd had with Mrs. Goodson of the state welfare department.

"In order to care for more than five children, you will need a child care institution license. Mrs. Goodson promised to report back to me and she hasn't," Chessie thought. Without delay she wrote a letter to the Division of Child Caring Institutions in Montgomery, requesting an appointment to discuss the requirements for setting up an institution. Communications rushed back and forth between Huntsville and Montgomery. Finally Chessie secured an appointment with a Mrs. Anthony in January 1955.

Never an ordinary woman, Chessie became extraordinary the day she drove alone to Montgomery and met with Mrs. Anthony. "I want to help children who are surviving by scavenging through waste containers, garbage cans, grocery store and hospital dumpsters," she pleaded.

Mrs. Anthony raised her eyes in astonishment. "We here in the state department are unaware of the conditions you're depicting. There may be a few isolated cases, but where is your

49

proof—your documentation? We need photographs or something to prove what you're saying is true. The minimum standards require that you provide documentation of the need for this service you propose to provide," Mrs. Anthony continued.

Chessie answered back. "I'm sure there's a great need for this service which would not only serve the Negro children in Madison County, but also any other county in Alabama. You see, Mrs. Anthony, I want to use my home as an institution for children," Chessie responded.

"Just how do you plan to finance your institution?" Mrs. Anthony wanted to know.

"Ma'am," Chessie spoke from her heart and hoped the lady was listening with hers. "I have enough love to help all the children in the streets of Huntsville. I have something to give that money can't buy. And I believe God works through people like you and me to supply their needs."

Mrs. Anthony cleared her throat. "Well, most institutions are financed by religious groups under the sponsorship of a board from each respective denomination."

"Well, I have not discussed this with the board of my church, but I will find a sponsoring organization," Chessie promised.

"Mrs. Harris," Mrs. Anthony said in closing the conversation, "It is important that you understand that you have to document the need. You must have a plan for financing, and the housing must meet requirements. An adequate staff is also necessary, and equipment must be up to par before you get a license as a child care institution. The requirements of the state are stringent. You might want to settle for your foster boarding license."

As she drove the 200 miles back home from Montgomery, Chessie had plenty of time to think. She didn't get much encouragement from Mrs. Anthony. But she was confident that she could meet the challenge of complying with all of the state requirements. Her unique personality would *never* take No for an answer to something that meant so much to her.

Upon returning home, Chessie scrounged around in her bedroom closet for an old camera the family hadn't used in years. She found it buried in a box of odds and ends.

A few days later she embarked on a photography tour. Armed with a purse full of film, she drove through inner city streets, through back alleys and deprived neighborhoods. There was no problem finding enough "evidence" to photograph. Chessie took many pictures. She found hungry children rummaging in garbage cans. She captured on film scenes of children sleeping in abandoned cars and on back porches. Many of the children knew her—some even took her to the filthy places they called home. She had earned access to their world of poverty.

But Chessie knew pictures would not be enough. Her next task was to prepare a written proposal of what she wanted to do and how it would be done. She spent hours preparing a concise and thorough report on the plight of street children.

With no formal college degree, Chessie trusted in God to help her put things down on paper in a professional and convincing manner.

A few weeks later, laden with the required evidence, Chessie again met with Mrs. Anthony.

"What I need from you now, Mrs. Anthony," she asserted as she handed her the photographs and well-written report, "are the legal requirements for a person to establish a child care institution." Chessie watched the woman's face carefully as she thumbed through the pictures and read the report. Visibly moved, Mrs. Anthony said, "All right, Mrs. Harris, you've convinced me. For starters you'll need a board of directors, a sponsoring organization, and we'll need all of this in writing. You'll need to bring your bank statement showing you have enough money to care for these children on an annual basis. The continuity of funding must be proved," Mrs. Anthony stated.

Chessie leaned forward in her chair, listening intently as she made notes: *board of directors, sponsoring organization, continuity of funding*. These words gathered like a detour on a highway. She prayed silently as she thought of how to remove these roadblocks, one by one.

After thinking for a moment, Chessie spoke with confidence in her voice. "The board of directors will be no problem. To show you my bankbook, well, I can do that now—because there's nothing in it. Money has nothing to do with care of children as I see it. You've said the state has no money to care for these children and I don't either, but I have a Father who does, and He will show me how to get it! I'll be back with all you are requiring."

Chessie left Mrs. Anthony sitting silently in her swivel chair watching as she left the office.

A year rolled by. Chessie prayed daily for God's guidance in meeting the requirements of the state for establishing a child care institution.

Although Chessie never doubted God, sometimes she wished He'd hurry and answer her prayer.

Sandwiched between her regular home duties and meal stops, Chessie continued the agonizing process of getting a board of directors together and finding a sponsoring organization. She made phone calls, personal visits, and even wrote a personal letter to the governor which read:

Dear Sir:

We are aware of the fact that we live in a desperately needy world. The anguished cry from those who are less fortunate than we rings constantly in our ears. The cry of the homeless Negro children has become so loud that it is extremely disturbing.

Two years ago my husband and I made it known to the welfare agencies of both here in our county and in the state department our deep desire to be of service in helping relieve this distress. We are happy to say that some good has been done, even though we have only touched it with our fingertips.

What we need in our state, Governor, is a home for our children. I am sure that you are aware that we do not have one of any type. If there ever was a need for one it is now.

We need your help. We are willing to offer our small two acres for full time service which is full of years of experience with working for and with children.

A word from you will be appreciated.
Sincerely, Chessie Harris

The Governor answered right back, offering encouraging words and requesting a report on her progress. However, in Chessie's ongoing dealings with the state, the caseworker emphasized over and over, "The need may not be as great as it may appear, and each child's case must be examined carefully by a caseworker before institutional care is established."

Chessie felt thoroughly frustrated at the denial of need. Although she sensed the officials' approval of her as a person, she also recognized their prejudice against accepting her as competent to handle the everyday problems of a child care institution. But she plodded on and decided to make an appeal to the community for financial support.

Chessie developed a brochure describing the needs of Huntsville's children. She arranged speaking engagements in local churches, at meetings of civic groups, on college campuses, and at Redstone Arsenal, a military installation. She developed a list of local church and civic leaders, local businessmen and professionals representing health education, mental health, and social service agencies. She systematically began contacting the people on her list, asking them to serve on the board of directors and inviting them to donate to the proposed child care institute. Each call was preceded by a prayer that God would give her the right words.

One afternoon she called a local businessman and said, "Mr. Rutledge, I'm calling to ask your help and support in establishing a home for neglected and dependent children." Chessie outlined her needs in detail. But his response, unfortunately, was typical of some she encountered.

"Well, Chessie, who else have you asked?" he said. After she told him, he replied curtly, "If those are the types of people you've contacted, I'd rather not serve."

Comments like these made her flinch in discomfort. But the most startling response came in writing from a respected community leader who said, "Well, you have the nerve, asking me to serve on the board of a home for colored children!"

Words of refusal bombarded Chessie's ears. Rejection was on every hand. She'd come so far.

Now it seemed her dreams lay shattered. To make matters worse, she received a terse letter from Mrs. Goodson at the State Welfare Department which read,

> *You are not authorized to solicit funds because you are not licensed by the state as a child care institution, but rather a foster boarding home licensed by the county DPS office.*
>
> *We urge you to stop all publicity and solicitation of funds.*

Chessie answered,

> *My intent has always been to stay within the law. My deep desire to see things go propelled me into action. I'll be ever so careful hereafter, you can be assured.*

Gradually, over several months, God clearly guided her to twelve individuals who finally said, "Yes, we'll be glad to serve on your board of directors."

Those accepting included an attorney, a judge, a minister, a businessman, a college president, a social worker, a doctor, and a housewife. Though a diverse group, they seemed to "click." After electing officers among themselves, the incorporation papers were drawn up by the attorney and probate judge. These wonderful volunteers officially became the board for Harris Home for Negro and Dependent Children. The first official board meeting was held December 13, 1956.

Chessie had every reason to be thrilled with her accomplishments thus far. But there was more work to be done. The part of herself that had a warm affinity for unloved children rejoiced in the success and also suffered in the knowledge of what was left to be done. Children all over Madison County were being mistreated. Would she ever be successful in helping them?

Chapter 9

Help Me, I'm Hurting

But whoso hath this world's good, and seeth his brother have need, and shutteth up his bowels of compassion from him, how dwelleth the love of God in him? My little children, let us not love in word, neither in tongue; but in deed and in truth (1 John 3:17, 18).

One chilly October morning, Chessie received a call from a nurse at the Madison County Health Department.

"I need someone to accompany me on a call this afternoon. Could you come? I don't want to go alone."

It took only fifteen minutes—driving down a country road—to reach their destination. Immediately, something that looked like a bag—a sack of potatoes or something lying in a ditch beside the road—caught the attention of the two women.

"Well, what is it?" Chessie strained to see as the bundle moved a bit. The two women drove up the dusty driveway, stopped, and got out of the car. The sight wasn't pretty. A dirty shack sat in the midst of trash, broken pieces of furniture, and junk of all types. By this time the object they'd seen in the ditch had moved to a woodpile near the house.

"Why, I believe it is a child," Chessie said, walking over to the small rag-wrapped bundle. It was a little girl. "Looks like she weights twenty-five pounds or less," Chessie thought. A matted burlap sack covered the child's scrawny body, and her face was scarred and covered with filth.

Chessie proceeded to investigate the child's condition further. As she bent down to touch the youngster, she noticed that her hands had developed a thick padding like an animal's hide. Bones protruded from the body, and the little bare feet were twisted grotesquely. An obnoxious odor exuded from the child. Upon closer examination Chessie discovered, to her horror, that the curly brown hair was matted with feces. All the filth—apparently months of accumulated dirt—combined to create an unbearable stench. The look in the child's eyes seemed to cry, "Help me, I'm hurting!"

As Chessie assessed the child's condition, the nurse went to the house to get as much background as possible. A heavy-set woman came out on the porch to talk, and Chessie listened as a sad story unfolded.

The child's mother died when she was born. The irresponsible father shirked his duty and distributed five motherless children among relatives and acquaintances. He supposedly went to another state to look for work. Unfortunately, he hadn't been heard from since.

The child, named Amy, was put outside in a pen with the household dogs and cats while the grownups worked the fields. This they considered protection and didn't realize the only learning she received was from the animals.

Chessie had seen terrible cases of neglect, but never anything like this. "Surely this child is an orphan of the living," she thought as she stood listening to this incredible story.

"Do you want to take this child home with you?" the nurse asked.

"Yes, I want her!" Chessie's voice was wrapped in compassion and heavy with emotion. She felt certain no one else would want the child because, first of all, there were no facilities in Alabama for black children, and, second, she felt certain most people would be unwilling to accept a child with the severe deprivation and problems this child obviously had.

With the utmost tenderness, Chessie picked the little girl up from the woodpile and carried her to the car. The stench was so terrible all the windows had to be rolled down.

After stopping at the Department of Social Services and taking care of the proper legal paperwork, Chessie began a careful deliberation. She knew that Amy would have to be soaked in something like detergent to remove the accumulated layers of filth.

"Where in the world did you get that child?" George exclaimed as Chessie carried her into the house.

"In the ditch," she answered. "Now I'm going to need a little help. So please run me a tub of warm water quickly. This child needs a bath!"

Marilyn and Joan, little mothers that they were, quickly pitched in to help. Soon it was apparent that Amy couldn't walk or talk. She cried and screamed, not like a human, but made sounds like those of dogs and cats whining.

"This will feel so nice," Chessie cooed as she peeled off the dirty rags and set Amy in the tub full of warm sudsy water. But the child stiffened. She resisted Chessie and the girls' touch and began screaming in a high-pitched moaning sound.

"This child has probably never had a bath," Chessie said to her daughters. "She's obviously not accustomed to being touched by humans either. And the sensation of water on her skin plus all this other handling is traumatizing." Chessie understood quite well the intense fear. Yet she knew they must continue the bath.

Many tubfuls of water later, Amy began to resemble a normal child. And to everyone's amazement, she had a gorgeous head of hair.

"She's really pretty, Mama," Joan said as she helped dry and dress the child in some clothing that Chessie kept downstairs for just such emergencies.

Getting Amy clean was minor compared to the problem of feeding her. Apparently she had developed the eating habits of an animal and was so malnourished that her digestive system wouldn't accept regular food. She'd vomit after eating anything except fruits or vegetables in their completely natural state—peels and all.

"This is the worst case of child abuse I've ever seen," the social worker said to Chessie when she called a few weeks later to see how the Harris family was getting along with Amy.

When Chessie thought of the circumstances leading to the

child's condition, her heart nearly broke. "How in the world did this child survive the neglect—living outside with animals?" Chessie thought.

"Do you think Amy will ever be normal, Mama?" Joan asked one day after Amy experienced a serious seizure.

Chessie optimistically answered her daughter. "I'm determined that Amy will learn—at least some basic skills."

Chessie worked with Amy day after day. The child had no sense of taste or smell. But she did respond to touch. When any member of the Harris family put their arms around her, Amy would smile and respond as a normal child. And within a few months she had begun to walk, in a waddling sort of way. Small successes. Gradual progress.

Chessie felt that Amy had potential and decided to take her to a children's clinic in Birmingham for evaluation.

"But we don't have extra money for this expense," George reminded Chessie one morning. "We're barely makin' it."

"Expensive medical care does seem out of reach," Chessie answered. "But somehow I feel if all of us sacrifice, we can get by." And the next week she began the 200-mile round trips to the clinic.

After many tests and several different evaluations, Amy's doctor broke the sad news to Chessie.

"Mother, your daughter's brain is not functioning. She has reached the peak of her capabilities and will never do any more than what she is now doing."

"I can't accept that prognosis, Doctor."

The physician tried to be kind, yet realistic. "Can't you see this child is never going to respond any more because her brain is not functioning?"

"Doctor, she's alive. As long as she lives let's keep trying. Maybe someday something will snap, and the child will be normal." Chessie's mind fought the truth.

Looking into Chessie's eyes with deep empathy, the doctor cautioned, "Mother, I want to warn you that one day when this child has a seizure, she will die. One of these onsets is going to be the last. I just want you to be prepared for that."

With a heavy heart Chessie took Amy back home, determined to continue helping her all she could.

Chessie was never prepared to accept the suffering of any child, and that is why she continued working hard to find a sponsoring organization—a group that would be responsible for funding.

By 1957 she had fine-tuned her appeal to the citizens of Huntsville. Armed with brochures, statistics, and a steel determination, she again made the rounds of church groups, clubs, business organizations, professional people, and ordinary citizens. So persuasive was her plea that the need was actually *felt* by many people who listened to her speak.

Mrs. Valene Battle was one of those whose heart was touched by the stories of the children. She found several other interested women, and together they made a special effort to meet Mrs. Harris and offer assistance.

One afternoon Chessie took them on a tour of the home, and they had the opportunity to hear the story of Amy and see the progress she had made. They saw other children staying in the Harris Home—some who merely needed love and affection. Then there were those children who had no homes, no security or love, little food and scant clothing.

"These poor children are given everything they need for proper development," Valene whispered to a friend as they continued their tour. The women's hearts were touched as they became aware of the plights of Huntsville's children whose parents just did not want them. And Chessie was quick to point out that there were many, many other children in the city and county who needed a place to go.

"There's no place in the whole state of Alabama for unwanted black children," Chessie emphasized as she summarized her plan of action to these women.

After seeing the children and talking together, the women knew that something had to be done to help Chessie meet the legal requirements to formally open an adequately staffed and furnished home for the children.

"The need is there, the home is offered, two kind people are offering their love, devotion, and effort. Surely we can do something to help," Valene challenged her friends.

The next week this concerned group of women met, discussed, and prayed for help in meeting the state requirements for a sponsoring organization. Because there was no such organization—one had to be created.

On June 10, four women met at the Church Street Community Center to set the framework for an organization which would serve as sponsor for the Harris Home. It was at this meeting that the Big Sister organization came into existence.

"We are alone in this project and cannot accomplish the purposes by ourselves," Valene challenged. So they sat down and wrote out their objectives: (1) to raise money to complete a much-needed remodeling and construction project on the Harris's personal home, and (2) to support the institution with funds until construction was completed. That day they left with the determination to see that the organization grew.

With hard work and sincerity the Big Sisters soon became officially recognized as the sponsoring organization under the auspices of the board of directors.

With joy in their hearts, the Harrises prayed for continued wisdom and guidance as they attempted to get licensed as a child care institution.

But before she could arrange another appointment with the child care institutions at Montgomery, Chessie received a call from Mrs. Bradshaw, the new director of the division.

"Could you meet with me here in Montgomery this week?" Mrs. Bradshaw inquired.

"I'm happy you called," Chessie said. "I was going to call you to set up a conference because I have all the things you need. I'm anxious to get my child care institutional license."

Upon arriving at the state capitol, Mrs. Bradshaw and Chessie were escorted into a large room. There were several distinguished men sitting around a well-polished conference table, all projecting an air of authority. Her initial confidence gave way to fright and intimidation.

The men were introduced as FBI agents.

"I wonder what FBI agents have to do with child care?" she questioned inwardly.

The men hurled question after question at Chessie. Though stunned, she answered concretely. Finally, one agent stated sternly, "We understand that you want to have a home for children. As long as you keep within the law with this children's home you won't hear from us. But we want you to know we will be watching every move you make."

What Chessie could not know or understand at the time was that the State Department wanted to make certain she was legitimate and had no self-serving motives. The men were introduced as FBI men to frighten Chessie.

Chessie thought to herself later, "There's no reason for those men to threaten me. I won't break any laws." However, one concern kept nagging her mind. What were the laws? She had never been given full guidelines for opening a child care institution.

Throughout the afternoon Chessie maintained her calm. She projected a businesslike image of firm confidence. Upon leaving the interrogation Chessie graciously said, "Thank you, gentlemen. Thank you very much."

As she and Mrs. Bradshaw left the room Chessie was not quite sure what she'd thanked the men for. She did realize they had not told her she couldn't start a child care institution. She felt that she had won her long-standing "battle" with the welfare department. She had been severely scrutinized, pushed to the limit. But she passed their examination with flying colors. She also recognized that it was the government's duty to make sure the little children she hoped to care for would not be placed in the hands of a fly-by-night operation.

After the two women were dismissed, Chessie followed Mrs. Bradshaw to her office and inquired, "Now, could you give me *in writing* the guidelines for my home?"

After some searching through her drawers and bookshelves, Mrs. Bradshaw handed Chessie a book entitled *Minimum Standards*. Chessie eagerly thumbed through the pages. She saw page after page of code citations and statutes governing the planned facilities for a child care institution. At last. Now she had some guidelines from which to work.

"Thank You, Lord," she whispered. "But where do I go from here?"

Chapter 10

Bulging at the Seams

Seek ye first the kingdom of God, and his righteousness; and all these things shall be added unto you (Matthew 6:33).

After going home and carefully reading the rules and regulations for obtaining a child care institution's license, Chessie realized there were some major projects which would need to be undertaken before she could ever expect to be licensed. More windows would be needed in some of the bedrooms, necessitating a large remodeling job. Bathrooms and kitchen facilities had to be enlarged, and there were numerous fire and safety codes that must be adhered to.

"We'll just have to raise the money." Chessie tried to be positive when talking with her board of directors and the Big Sisters.

At their next meeting the Big Sisters began laying plans for raising the necessary funds to remodel Chessie's four-bedroom home. They organized Mother's Day flower sales, Bar-B-Que sales, sale of a calf, sale of tickets for a new little red sports car donated by an interested businessman—even a beauty contest to choose "Miss Spring." There were telethons, talent shows, and a host of creative fund-raising projects.

Sandwiched between fund raising, managing the house, and various business dealings, Chessie worked hard to make sure their home was a place of comfort and love. George was such a support! How grateful she felt for his willing help. Yet a nagging concern flickered within her heart whenever she thought of their finances and the overcrowding in the house. Sometimes there were close to twenty children living in the four-bedroom brick dwelling. With so many of them needing things and her no longer working at a regular job, cash flow was low. And the funds coming in from the Big Sisters' efforts were designated for specific projects and could not be touched for personal use.

When she and George talked about how to come up with more money, they always ended up deciding to dig deeper into their own resources. But there was a limit to how much they could do.

Chessie could sit only so many hours at the sewing machine. And even though they canned, preserved, and cooked the majority of their meals from home-grown produce, still there were things that only cash could provide.

Chessie and George began praying earnestly for guidance and help as they sought to enlarge the facilities and move closer to obtaining their child care license. One thing was certain—they must begin the addition on their home soon.

One night, after adding up some outstanding bills, George said, "Times is tight, Honey. We're not makin' much headway financially. What would you think if I went back to my factory job in Cleveland?"

Chessie didn't know what to think. She didn't want George away from the family. But, realistically, she faced the fact that if they were going to continue pressing toward their goal, they needed more money.

After thinking it over, George wasn't totally convinced it was God's will for him to leave his family and go to a distant city to work. George knew he was needed around the house. Besides, he had heard that jobs up north were scarce. He continued to pray and ask God's guidance.

Every night for several weeks he earnestly petitioned the Lord in prayer. Then one Monday evening he prayed, "Lord, I'm askin' for a sign. If you want me to go, help me sell my car—*tomorrow*."

The next day, before George returned home from work and cleaned up, four people came to buy his car. "That's a miracle—a sure sign." He smiled at Chessie.

Within a week George collected his things and on a Sunday afternoon, he left Huntsville on a bus bound for Cleveland.

He wasted no time in getting to the factory where he had been previously employed. After arriving, he immediately asked to see the president. Just back from lunch, the man ushered George into his office.

"I hear you want your job back, Harris."

"Yes, sir."

"Well, the president before me always said, 'If a man ever quits, don't ever hire him back.' "

George thought a moment and answered, "But sir, I didn't quit to work for another company. I worked here twenty-five years—there's nothing in that galvanizing department I can't do."

The president leaned forward, folded his hands, and confided, "Harris, I think I'll handle this situation the way the foreman would. I'm not only gonna give you your job back, but I'll start you off at $1.90 an hour."

"Praise God!" George thought in his heart. Then he thanked the president and hurried to his little rented room to write Chessie. This was more money than he'd ever made before. And he promised to send most of it back home every week.

During the first weeks after George left, Chessie felt overwhelmed with the responsibilities of caring for more than twenty children. George, her loyal supporter, always working beside her, played a valuable role. He supported her drive to help the children, and his absence made a gigantic gap in the family unit.

With few resources, she gathered her courage and thought carefully how she would manage.

First of all, her daily schedule had been an outstanding success when they had fewer than eight children. Now that the family bulged at the seams, the values of organization, agendas, and thoroughness were never more needed or appreciated. A typical day went something like this:

5:00 A.M.—Wake-up time. Chessie insisted that waking up

be a happy time—one of pleasant memories. She would sing in her clear soprano voice:

Lord, in the morning Thou shalt hear
　　My voice ascending high;
To Thee will I direct my prayer,
　　To Thee lift up mine eye.

O may Thy Spirit guide my feet
　　In ways of righteousness;
make every path of duty straight
　　And plain before my face.

Then she'd call sweetly, "Are you up, Girls? Come on, Boys, let's move now. It's another day." Then sleepy-eyed children would hurry to the bathroom to wash and groom themselves. Returning to their rooms, they made the beds and tidied up.

At 5:30 the kitchen crew moved into action. Every child was responsible for something. Each had a specific job assigned once a week during the family-council sessions.

While the kitchen crew started breakfast, those responsible for laundry scurried with their baskets of soiled clothes into the laundry room. Those assigned household duties began sweeping, dusting, and putting things away. Throughout the house children's voices could be heard chanting the little rhyming verses Chessie taught them to help them understand the importance of doing their jobs to the best of their abilities: "All you do, do it with your might; things done by half, are not done right."

6:10 A.M.—Breakfast. The first meal of the day was often quite an ordeal because eating in the morning was something new for many of the children. Not accustomed to a nourishing, well-balanced meal so early, some of them resisted. But Chessie won them over. Her carefully planned menus included fruit or juice, hot cereal if the weather was cold—cold cereal if it was hot, some type of protein, scrambled eggs, and hot biscuits. And there was always an abundance of fresh, cold milk.

Chessie made sure there was plenty of everything—more

than the children could possibly eat. She delighted in observing the joy sweeping over little faces when children knew there was lots of food and they did not have to skimp.

6:45 A.M.—Preparation for school. The older children helped the younger ones gather their supplies and books for school, making sure all the homework was collected so that by 7:00 A.M. everyone would be out in front of the house to meet the school bus.

7:15 A.M.—A quiet house. Chessie now focused all her attention on the babies, making sure they were comfortable. In between caring for them, she spent the remainder of the day doing the typical "mother" jobs—cooking, sewing, planning, running errands, etc.

3:00 P.M.—Children arrive home from school. When the school bus unloaded its precious cargo, everyone made a dash for the kitchen, where a delicious snack awaited. Many times the house was perfumed with the aroma of freshly baked bread, cinnamon rolls, or cupcakes. Then Mama Harris sat at the large wooden table and listened to the tales of what happened that day at school, on the bus, or what teacher had been unfair or especially good that day! She heard the unspoken needs, she calmed the childish fears, and sometimes she actually took notes of things the children told her so they could all discuss it again in the family hour before bedtime.

4:00 P.M.—Free time. This happy break from the daily regimen allowed each child to do whatever he or she wished. They played ball, wandered outside in the yard, played tag, wrote letters, or visited with friends.

6:00 P.M.—Supper preparation. Chessie's delicious meals drew even an uncooperative child inside at supper time. The older children assisted the younger ones in washing hands, brushing hair, or cleaning mud and grass off clothes.

6:25 P.M.—Supper. What an inviting time! A typical evening meal included a good meat loaf, mashed potatoes, greens, raw carrots, celery sticks, homemade bread, margarine, and milk. Occasionally, when Chessie had time to bake, there would be a deep-dish apple pie with tender, flaky crust, or some other luscious dessert. Most of the meals were prepared a day ahead by the very organized kitchen crew. Things went like clockwork. Everyone helped. When there were more than ten children, they ate in shifts with the smaller ones served first.

Duties were assigned on a regular basis, and after-supper jobs included washing dishes, removal of trash, feeding of animals, and sweeping the floors. All of these assignments were made on a weekly basis in the family hour held after supper.

7:00 P.M.—Family worship. After a busy day the little brood gathered each evening for a special worship hour and family discussion time. Honoring God first with songs, stories, and prayers, they closed the session by discussing various problems that might have arisen during the day.

For example, if Chessie noticed a child complaining about something at school, this was brought up and talked out. Bible memory work was stressed, and the children learned the Beatitudes, Ten Commandments, and other significant Scripture verses.

7:30 P.M.—Quiet time. This part of the evening was spent in study, reading, or working on quiet projects.

8:45-9:30 P.M.—Bath time. The younger children got their baths first, assisted by the older ones. By 9:30 everyone was to be bathed, in their night clothes, and quiet.

10:00 P.M.—Lights Out. Some nights after Chessie went to bed and the house was quiet and still, she'd lie awake thinking, planning, dreaming. Pondering the day's decisions, she reflected on the relationships solidified, the hearts touched, the characters developed. As thoughts twirled in her head at two, three, or even four in the morning, she often slipped quietly out of bed, fell on her knees, and talked with Her Counselor, her Source of strength and courage.

Chessie recognized that the practical, material things she gave children—such as good meals, a secure home environment, and comfortable beds—made children feel more human and helped them control their behavior and actions. But she also wanted to give them the greatest gift of all—the opportunity of accepting Jesus as their personal Saviour.

Chapter 11

Together Again

Trust in the Lord, and do good; so shalt thou dwell in the land, and verily thou shalt be fed. Delight thyself also in the Lord; and he shall give thee the desires of thine heart. Commit thy way unto the Lord; trust also in him; and he shall bring it to pass (Psalm 37:3-5).

Two years swept by. Chessie and the children managed quite well even with George away. His paycheck supported twenty-six people. Yet Chessie missed him terribly! She longed for his presence and companionship. She realized the need of his expertise and authority around the house. "I must persuade him to return home soon," she decided.

Meanwhile in Cleveland the two years seemed like an eternity to George. One evening he sat down to write to Chessie. *"Even though I'm sending money back to all of you, it hurts me to realize the children are growing and will soon be out on their own. I feel I'm missing out on so much of their lives, and besides, I miss Jay so much."* How George wanted to hug and kiss the little foster baby with the curly red hair. After receiving the letter, Chessie determined in her heart that George must return home. And she began encouraging him. Answering one of her letters he said, *"I've worked for the company a total of twenty-seven years. I sorta' feel indebted to the president for giving me my job back. I'm ashamed to tell the boss I want to leave again."*

And yet, George felt a growing conviction of his duty to the family. He knew that money could never provide emotional support, caring, and loving concern. He knew what he must do, and it wasn't long before he was on a bus headed for Huntsville.

When he walked in the door, everyone dropped what they were doing and one by one, the children who remembered George threw their arms around his neck, hugging and kissing him. As he greeted each child he inquired, "Where's that little baby Jay?" He felt so eager to hold the little boy in his arms again.

Joan sidled up to her father and spoke hesitantly.

"Someone adopted him, Papa."

"You mean the baby is gone—adopted?" George felt his heart lurch. He looked over at Chessie, who stood in the kitchen door, her eyes filled with compassion.

"What happened to my baby, Honey?" George felt a lump filling his throat. "Nothin' in the world hurts me worse than knowin' that baby's gone."

Later, as they talked things over in the privacy of their little room, George and Chessie discussed the reality of taking foster children and then seeing them either returned to their biological parents or adopted. In his heart George recognized that Jay, in all probability, would benefit from the adoption. Yet he felt a deep wound in his spirit because he had looked forward to reestablishing a close relationship with the little boy. But in spite of the pain, he knew there were other children who needed his love.

George had been home just three days when a letter arrived from the president of the galvanizing company in Cleveland.

"George, I'm sorry you didn't feel you could talk to me about leaving your job. I understand and I'm sorry to see you go."

George appreciated the kind words. Yet he didn't regret his decision to return home. He felt needed. He knew he had made the right decision.

Chapter 12

Lessons in Living

If ye abide in me, and my words abide in you, ye shall ask what ye will, and it shall be done unto you (John 15:7).

With George home and his paycheck gone, finances were once again very tight. But the little flock found solace in each other when times were tough. Chessie and George tried to reinforce over and over the principles of "We *can* do it; we can *work* together; we can *pray* together; we can *talk* together; we can *make decisions* together; *WE CAN MAKE IT!* Together, we can do *anything!*"

By the end of 1959 the Big Sisters had taken over much of the major load of fund raising, freeing Chessie to devote more time to her goal of opening the child care institution.

George shouldered a share of the household responsibilities, kept her car in good working order, and had a tremendous rapport with the boys in residence. His presence took a great load off his wife's mind, giving her more time to finalize plans for the addition on their overcrowded house.

In every bedroom there were at least three bunk beds, and any new children slept in comfortable pallets on the floor. Siblings of the same sex shared a twin bed—one child at the head and the other at the foot.

"I've never seen so many bunks in my life," George laughed one morning, as he helped a young man tidy up his room. This particular boy had been referred by the local welfare department until his run-away mother could be located.

Chessie never tried to turn anyone away who needed immediate care. Yet, realistically, there was no room for more children. And the financial obligations for twenty-six people were staggering. It soon became apparent that unless everyone got involved in fund raising, they weren't going to make it. A formidable challenge—but they faced it squarely and rose to the occasion.

George organized the boys and taught them how to grow fruits and vegetables that quickly gained a reputation for being "the best in town." His garden services were in demand. He planted a garden for anyone who wanted one but did not have time to do the work.

The family set up a roadside stand manned by some of the more responsible children. They did a thriving business. This, of course, wasn't a guaranteed year-round income. But it proved successful in the growing season.

Subsequently, Chessie decided to sell her ability to cook. She began preparing homemade meals and selling them to nearby construction workers. Her fried chicken, potato salad, garden fresh vegetables, fresh hot biscuits, and luscious fruit pies generated a regular clientele.

Teaching the children to generate funds became Chessie's consuming passion. "You must learn to become self-sufficient," she said. "And never, never be without a dime in your pocket."

Chessie taught them to sell candy, greeting cards, and other items that could be peddled from door to door. From the moment children came to the Harris Home, they learned the importance of work.

"You have to do something. You can't come to Harris Home, sit down and be president, walk around, talk big and do nothing," George instructed. And for practical help he and Chessie taught the importance of thrift-buying at a discount, then selling for a profit.

In the summer, George purchased old lawn mowers, repaired them, and helped the boys find jobs grooming lawns. The kids grew proficient at trimming hedges, taking care of bushes, and edging grass. Their attention to detail won them more jobs and a sterling reputation for excellence in the community.

One winter when a ferocious ice-and-snow storm struck, the Harris family boys were the first ones out with snow shovels, offering to clean driveways and walks. People paid as much as $6.00 a driveway—unheard of pay in those days.

Some of the children made enough money to buy their own clothes. Others had a sufficient amount for pocket change. Chessie and George never kept the money the children earned for themselves. If a child made $4.00 a day, he could keep $2.00. The remainder went in the bank. When the children grew older, became more responsible, or when it was time to leave the home, they had a little "nest egg" built up to tide them over until they found a good job.

Some of the children possessed firmly entrenched tendencies to evil. Chessie worked hard to help them learn of a loving God whose power to change hearts is unsurpassed.

The Harris family team taught by example the importance of church attendance. When the children of Harris Home started down the hill of their property to walk to the nearby church, neighbors remarked, "Look, here comes the Harris family!" The group usually filled four or five pews in the sanctuary. All the foster children, regardless of previous environment and social structure, fit right in. They didn't feel strange because they'd learned manners and social graces at Harris Home before going out in public.

Because the somewhat chaotic lives of street children provided no natural rhythm of learning, Chessie recognized their desperate need of God to help change inherited and environmental characteristics. As she worked with them, day by day she saw on their faces the intense longing inside their souls for something better. And she ever sought to point the children to their heavenly Father. Bringing a child to Christ thrilled Chessie to unutterable heights. One boy's prayer forever echoed in her mind.

"God, I thank Thee for bringing me to this place. 'Cause down yonder I never knowed about You."

The difference Christ made in a troubled life became obvious as little hearts responded to the Holy Spirit. As a young person learned to talk with Jesus, his life radiated a new brightness. His life became lighter, and a new serenity replaced the old doubts and fears.

"Children, you can't get along without prayer in your life—at least not successfully," George said. And the kids knew the Bible was true because George said so! He treated the children with such kindness and love that their hearts were openly drawn to "George's God." George had the precious ability to weave religion into the fabric of everyday work. He had many chances to teach the children eternal values as they worked together raising their own chickens, cows, and working in their huge garden.

About this time, Chessie providentially heard of an old building called Butler Hall on the Oakwood College campus that was to be torn down. The family immediately contacted those in charge and made a proposal. "We're willing to tear down the building if you will give us the materials as payment for our labor."

A deal was struck. Strong wood of excellent quality provided just the start they needed to get going. Soon hammers were ringing and saws were buzzing. Chessie and George had many talents between them, but the job of tearing down Butler Hall proved to be a major undertaking! Something for which they were really unprepared.

It turned out to be a circus—like building the tower of Babel. They had plenty of helpful volunteers, but there weren't any experts who could take charge. Chessie tried to act as overseer, and marshaled her little army to help. But frankly, it was chaos. In due time, however, the job was finished and they had a good supply of lumber.

Tearing down the building, they soon discovered, was the easy part! Designing and constructing a good-looking addition to their house was the next challenge. Chessie constantly communicated her desire to have a big enough place to get a child care institute license.

"We can do it! We can do it! We can work together!" was the group's theme. They had little money and no choice but to try and do the work themselves with the help of volunteers from the community.

When it came time to put up sheetrock, however, they had completely run out of money.

"We'll do it ourselves," Chessie asserted. They did, but after they completed the job it looked so bad that Chessie had to shut the door and pray, "Lord, this looks terrible. Won't you send somebody to fix it and get it ready for the painters?"

The next morning a man knocked on the door and said, "I understand you are opening a home for children. I'm interested and want to help out. I don't have much money, but I'm a painter and I put up sheetrock and strip it."

Stunned for moment, Chessie regained her composure and then grinned broadly. "Come in, Sir. You are heaven sent."

Another construction disaster occurred when a gentleman who volunteered to put in some windows, put them all in upside down!

"I could be upset," Chessie sighed to George. "But I'm just going to trust the Lord and thank Him for this trial. There must be something He wants me to learn from this disaster. And she held her patience every time she rolled the window the opposite way to open it.

They did as much as they could with the cash they had managed to scrape together, but before the much-needed addition to their house could be finished, they again ran out of money.

"I'm not giving up," Chessie said. "I know somewhere God has available funds for us. All I have to do is find it."

After much deliberation and prayer, she felt impressed to contact the president of a local bank for a loan. He told her to bring in the estimate on the unfinished work, plus any outstanding bills, and the bank would take a first mortgage. Feeling grateful, Chessie totaled their needs and came up with the figure of $7,500. She felt happy as she hurried to the bank on a sunny Monday morning. After waiting a few minutes to see the banker, Chessie was ushered into his plush office.

The businessman scrutinized the itemized statement and carefully looked over the bills before blurting, "I didn't know you were going to build a mansion for beggars." His insensitivity stabbed her heart and filled her eyes with pain. "There's no way that we want to take a mortgage on this building," the banker's words sounded final.

Praying silently, Chessie left his office undaunted. Coming out of the building into the morning sun she began walking down the sidewalk. Continuing to pray, she told the Lord, "I can't go home and tell George and all these children there's no money." Almost as if someone answered out loud, the words came to her mind, "Keep walking."

Obediently she continued down the street. Soon she stood in front of a three-story brick office building. Again, a conviction stronger than ever said, "Take the elevator to the third floor." She did and found herself in the office of an attorney whom she had never seen.

Quickly, she spilled her story of need. The attorney appeared genuinely angered by the banker's behavior as Chessie related what had just happened. With a flushed face he leaned forward and said, "You go on back home. We will be out there this afternoon to see what you are doing."

"Thank You, Jesus." Chessie breathed a silent prayer of joy as she left the office and hurried home.

That afternoon, a long, sleek black car rolled up to the Harris Home. The vehicle stopped, and the three official-looking gentlemen stepped out. After greeting them, Chessie gave them a tour, all the while briefing them on the future plans and needs.

After going through each room, the attorney she had spoken to in the office stated, "You have done a terrific job here. Will $7,500 be enough to finish?"

Chessie was speechless. The exact amount they needed— how good God is! Chessie quickly recovered her composure and answered, "Yes, Sir, thank you very much!"

The next day she returned to the attorney's office and picked up the check.

"Thank You, Lord, for removing more roadblocks," Chessie praised her heavenly Father in gratitude.

Yet she knew there were more children out there needing help.

Chapter 13

They Cared Enough to Share

The Lord giveth wisdom: out of his mouth cometh knowledge and understanding (Proverbs 2:6).

———————

"If it weren't for your assistance, I don't know how we'd ever manage financially," Chessie remarked to the ten women assembled for a Big Sister's meeting one afternoon.

"We're glad to help and we'll do all we can," the president of the group answered. And true to their commitment, these dedicated women raised over $10,000 in one year's time and worked untiringly to do whatever they could for the children coming to Harris Home.

The Big Sisters accomplished what Chessie couldn't. They provided summer vacations in their homes, took the children to church on special days such as Christmas and Easter, and even sacrificed their own personal resources and purchased clothing for the children. When there was an urgent need for kitchenware or linens, the Big Sisters came to the rescue.

Finally, after three long years, the red brick house had a six-bedroom addition and was up to code. Now Chessie concentrated more of her energy on completing final requirements for her institutional license, which mainly involved organizing the financial end of the home.

As she dealt with bureaucrats on a regular basis, Chessie saw the wisdom in improving herself academically, feeling that if she had some college credits in early childhood education and adolescent psychology, she'd have more to offer.

She enrolled at the University of North Carolina and St. Louis University during the summer months while George supervised the home. Their own four children, now nearing their twenties, worked beside their father and carried as much of the load as they could.

Each Harris child had a unique personality and possessed different abilities that contributed to the smooth running of what was now a serious family business.

"Lord, I thank You for the children you've given us and for their talents of management, bookkeeping, secretarial skills, and communication," Chessie prayed one evening. "And I thank You, too, for the opportunity to study and enhance my abilities."

It was now 1960 and funds were running dangerously low. Chessie wisely recognized that in order for the home to grow and be recognized as legitimate, it would have to give up its "mom and pop" status and become a full-fledged, non-profit business. But where could she get funding?

One Friday evening, Chessie sat on the front porch of the remodeled brick home. Her eyes moved to the horizon and the swell of distant hills. The sweet sound of organ music from the church's Friday night vesper service drifted to her ears on the early-evening breeze. Nearby, a group of rosebushes, lush with blossoms, perfumed the air. She felt drawn to God.

"Lord," she breathed an earnest prayer, "please show me where to get the money to prove a continuity of funding."

Suddenly, an idea popped into her mind. "The United Givers' Fund! Why haven't I thought of that before?" Chessie knew that funds from the United Way were given to worthy organizations filling a need in the community.

"Why can't we appeal to this organization?" she mused "The worst thing that could happen would be they would say No!"

The next Monday, Chessie began to outline a plan. She again had a little brochure printed describing the past progress and future needs of Harris Home. Anything she could do to enhance the public's awareness of her home, she did. She contacted businesses, made herself available to speak at various functions around town, and prayed earnestly that God would bless her efforts.

After months of hard work, she made an appointment with the director of the United Givers' fund to request becoming a part of the fund system. He explained the policy of providing them with a CPA audit for the past year and a projected future budget. "A citizens review committee will make the final decision," he said. "This process of consensus takes six to eight months."

"Well, we'll just wait and hope for the best," Chessie answered confidently.

In the meantime, she used all her ingenuity to raise funds. One businessman, the owner of a motel said, "We get a lot of requests for free things, Chessie, that we would enjoy sharing with your children."

This particular gentleman sponsored many banquets at which there was often left-over food. Because Chessie let the need be known, the surplus of food was donated to Harris Home—a tremendous savings on the grocery budget of their growing family.

Another man, when asked why he donated items to the Home said, "She comes across as you might look at your grandmother. It's hard to turn your grandmother down!"

Articulating the common needs in uncommon ways nearly always uncovered the essential goodness and compassion in the people Chessie approached. And she was careful about the way she went about publicizing the need. As a black woman, she felt the yoke of racism heavily weighted with the culture of poverty and misery. She constantly rose above the unskilled and uneducated view of her race that many whites held of all blacks.

With a bold courage and firm courtesy, Chessie continued to search for help. And she needed courage because the reality of the times included the bombing of black churches, vicious beatings of blacks by the Ku Klux Klan or racist whites, attacks by police dogs, and white firemen dispersing crowds of protesting black men, women, and children with blasts from powerful water hoses. The civil rights movement progressed painfully as innocent, law-abiding black citizens were humiliated, degraded, and often treated less than human in their struggle for equality.

However, Chessie did a masterful job of avoiding controversy and bureaucratic bickering. She used her impeccable manners when dealing with people. Her sharp mind and articulate speech persuaded many a dubious contributor. Although Chessie was at a disadvantage during the controversy of these years—years tragically dividing the American people—she always sought to see the best in people. She set out to prove in a simple and straightforward manner that black children shouldn't suffer—that children, no matter what color, did not deserve discrimination and insult, as no one did.

But the idea of racial superiority and segregation ruled in Alabama. In many situations the relationship between blacks and whites was still that of master and servant. And Chessie recognized the role racism played in the neglect of little children. A lack of hope and jobs for young black men translated into frustration at being unable to take responsibility for the children they fathered. Men, unable to maintain themselves in the labor force, were unable to maintain their families.

Throughout this dreadful time of civil unrest and hate, Chessie determined more than ever to keep moving ahead with her plans for a children's home.

"I may not be able to do anything about past discrimination," she thought, "but at least I can attempt to change the direction of the next generation."

One morning in 1960, Chessie went to the mailbox and found a letter from the United Givers' Fund of Huntsville. She eagerly tore open the envelope and read, *We are happy to inform you that Harris Home has been accepted for funding beginning January 1 with an annual budget of $12,500.*

Joyfully, Chessie gathered the family for worship that evening, and together they praised God for the new avenue of funding.

Although this money covered the running costs, it didn't provide the capital funds needed for expansion. However, consistent funding did ease the tension of trying to provide the basic necessities for the many children in the home. With a determined heart, Chessie went on soliciting support, but gradually, individual contributions began to wane. People thought the United Way money was enough.

"Have you ever tried to maintain a home—feed, clothe, and educate more than twenty-six people, for $12,500 a year?" Chessie pointed out to a former contributor. The need for free-will contributions was obvious and Chessie still regularly hounded the state welfare office about her institutional license. Her mind set didn't allow her to take No for an answer. "I will provide the best legal care for Alabama's children with the help of God," she vowed.

How thankful she was, however, for the regular income they received from the local United Way. Now she did not have to expend so much mental energy on fund raising and could better concentrate on meeting the pressing needs of the children.

One continuing problem came from the fact that some of the children coming to the home had not attended school on a regular basis. They were culturally and academically deprived. They were unaware of many things society takes for granted.

For example, some of the children, when initiated into a regular school program, weren't comfortable with activities involving discipline and learning. Torn from unstructured lives of chaos, they didn't like having to sit still in school, being with lots of children frequently younger than they were, or being told what to do by teachers and principals.

"It's going to be a real challenge for me to change this ingrained behavior," Chessie told her daughters, Marilyn and Joan. "We must find ways to help these children to *like* learning!"

Chessie sought God's help in this matter, and it wasn't long before she hit upon an idea. One day she said to George, "I've decided to start my own little home school right here. We'll move all the furniture out of the downstairs recreation room and make it into a schoolroom-library."

Chessie knew Alabama State Law stipulated that children must be in school. To deliberately keep them out was a crime.

However, she decided to press her luck in keeping some of the "harder-to-manage" children home three days, and then sending them to school a day or two. If the children showed progress, she would know the plan worked.

She tried it, and the system proved effective. Chessie stuck to simple teaching at home. She helped the children learn the ABC's, how to count, and encouraged them to sit still and listen. All this was done by story telling, sprinkled with lots of love and positive reinforcement.

"Oh, my precious child, how well you did today!" She'd repeat to each and every one, over and over. "I'm so glad you can count to ten now—I'm so proud of you!" This affirmation made the children's hearts swell with pride and they worked hard to do better next time.

As the home school met with astounding success, Chessie began enlisting volunteers from Oakwood College and the A & M College nearby to come and help with the children. She instructed her youthful helpers carefully. "If you get a 'bad' child, set him on your lap so he can feel your love. Hug him tightly. This way he'll understand there is someone who really cares."

Chessie understood that when children feel lonely and think nobody cares, they can't learn. And to know that someone will offer support means everything to a child.

Some of the bright, eager children advanced quickly. One exceptional group of children took a whole grade during the summer with the help of a volunteer teacher. And at the end of the fall, they were promoted to the next grade with a "B" average. How wonderful they felt about themselves!

"Feeling good about yourself is important," Chessie told her own daughters. And together the three of them worked hard to help the children by teaching them good grooming habits.

The children's self-esteem soared as they were taught how to look and smell nice. For "pretty is as pretty does," Chessie often told them. Every Sabbath morning before church, the children were required to march by Chessie's door—showing off shoes, hair, and clothes so as to be appropriate for church. Some youngsters had never been "dressed up" in church clothing before.

And speaking of clothing, shopping for the kids was no small challenge. This type of excursion, which usually included more than fifteen children, necessitated careful planning.

Often, during an advertised sale at Sears, Penneys, or Montgomery Ward, Chessie made arrangements to bring her brood in either before the store officially opened, or after closing. That way the clerks could assist in the buying process. How proud the children were when they returned home with a brand new outfit—not a hand-me-down!

However excited the children felt about new clothing, the best part of being at Harris Home was the feeling of "being safe."

"You can just be yourself, and I will always love you, no matter what," Chessie emphasized often in the family-council sessions. And with joy she watched the relief on faces previously etched with worry and pain. The security of having one's own bed, lots of friends, and plenty of personal attention plus regular nutritious meals, made worlds of difference in the outlook and attitude of neglected and abused children.

Relating properly to one's peers took hours of training. Chessie spent much time instructing the children on proper social behavior, good manners, and the rules of dating. They talked everything out—discussed over and over the details of a "tasteful" life. Chessie felt the girls and boys under age sixteen should be chaperoned when going out on dates. One day she discerned resistance to her ideas and decided to find out why.

After a bit of discussion in the family-council hour, one of the girls spoke up and said, "Mama, it just kind of makes us feel funny for you to take us to parties and come back and pick us up. We just wondered if we could go by ourselves."

Chessie then had the opportunity to explain how she was responsible for their safety. Many of them had never known about the laws of insurance and the liability if someone were hurt in an accident. And so, together that evening they decided that Thursday evening would be "date night." And everybody was expected to be home by 9:30 p.m.

Chessie helped the young people plan exactly what to do on

a date. She cautioned them on kissing and being obnoxious and immoral. They all role-played and learned to plan ahead exactly what to do so there would be little opportunity for temptation. "This way," Chessie reminded the children, "you'll never have to worry about guilt feelings."

The date night was a smashing success. The family continued to encourage an open dialogue with each other. There was absolutely NOTHING they could not sit down and discuss very openly. And this commitment to openness proved again and again to be a source of strength, solace, and comfort to each family member.

Life in their home was becoming increasingly congested. With more and more children constantly coming and going, Chessie felt the need to stress privacy for the girls and boys. To accomplish this, she decided to rearrange the house so that the girls lived on one side, with her and Georges' room in the middle, and the boys on the other. And never the twain should meet!

Occasionally, some daring teen would attempt to break a rule. But Chessie was firm and did not allow anyone to enter the restricted area of the opposite sex. If they did, they were severely punished. When administrating discipline, Chessie always sought God's guidance because her goal was not to punish, but to help children see that they must never repeat the offensive behavior.

Things were now running along quite smoothly. And how thankful Chessie and George were for United Way's support. But the children kept coming.

Chessie ever attempted to convey to the children that her own resource and motivation to help them came from heaven above.

And she needed much patience and wisdom as she sought to change the life direction of so many children. She had worked long and hard and had seen many results; yet she still lacked an institutional license. Would she ever succeed?

Chapter 14

Love Unlocked the Door

But thou, when thou prayest, enter into thy closet, and when thou hast shut thy door, pray to thy Father which is in secret; and thy Father which seeth in secret shall reward thee openly (Matthew 6:6).

September of 1960 rolled into October, and an Indian summer stretched out warm and lazy across the Alabama countryside.

One afternoon a caseworker from the state department of welfare called on Chessie. Together they toured the home, the worker asking many questions and taking notes. Before leaving she confided, "Chessie, our committee is meeting in early December to discuss your licensing. I'm going to recommend that you get it! But, one thing I'd advise is it might be wise for you to consider forming satellite homes in the near future, instead of enlarging your present facility, and hiring more people to help you."

Chessie felt a rush of excitement welling up inside. Was her dream about to become a reality? The reality of her world included children—children coming from many difficult situations. She would have to wait a little longer before celebrating.

One day she received a call from a social worker at the county welfare department.

"Chessie, I have six children. We must get them out of their house this weekend. Can you take them?"

Chessie's mind began to spin. "Where will I put six more children? We're so full!"

They were always full. But Chessie knew she could not turn these little ones away. And so, on a busy Friday afternoon around three-thirty they arrived. Chessie, as usual, was ready. The beds were made and clothes picked out for four little sisters ages four, six, nine, and twelve. The boys were ten and eleven.

Before the children arrived, Chessie closeted herself away for a couple of hours of earnest prayer. This was her policy when new ones came—to try and find as much of Jesus as she could, because it took a great deal of compassion and patience to deal with children ripped from their familiar surroundings.

As the social worker's car pulled into the driveway, Chessie looked out the window. Immediately her heart filled with gloom because as the car door opened the little feet reluctantly began to come out; she saw four blue-eyed, stringy-haired girls and two little boys who were trying to pull up what had been britches. How would these white children relate to her and the other kids?

Opening the front door, Chessie stepped outside and opened her arms wide, praying all the time that the little group would accept the love the Harris family freely offered.

The children moved slowly toward her. One of the little sisters pulled the other one back, but Chessie coaxed, "Come on, come on." They began to take baby steps and finally got close enough for Chessie to touch them. With a smile on her face, she reached first for the four-year-old, who was trembling. She wrapped her arms around the little one and drew her tight. As she held the child close she could feel the little one's heart beating faster and faster. And as Chessie looked up at the other children, she could read the questions in their eyes.

"I wish I had a thousand arms," Chessie thought as she let loose of the little girl. She wanted to hold them all, one by one, but she could see the terror on the youngest one's face. She kept one arm around the child while moving as close as possible to the others, patting them gently and comforting them as best she could. They could not possibly know how much she would love them.

The social worker stood by the car with tears in his eyes. This was his first experience working with a black woman, and his heart flooded with a strange compassion and amazement as he watched Chessie wrap her arms of love around these needy white children.

"We have a problem," the worker hesitated. "There are so few clothes for them, and I don't know how you'll manage."

"Don't worry," Chessie assured him. "We always have extra clothes. But first, they'll need a bath."

In a little while all six children were scrubbed clean; with fresh clothes on and after a good night's rest, their little faces brightened considerably. The trauma of being shifted to a new home gradually wore off as they experienced affection and loving care from the Harris family.

The social worker regularly checked on the children and in a letter to Chessie the next month he said, *I have never placed children in a place where there is more warmth and love than yours.*

And as Chessie became more familiar with the children's ugly past of sexual and emotional mistreatment, she prayed with them and assured them that God would take care of their needs and that she loved them too.

Eventually the six children were placed in other homes, but Chessie felt satisfied that she had provided a temporary refuge from abuse and pain and that a door of hope and love was opened.

The months rolled on. Christmas of 1960 came and went.

By this time Chessie had hired helpers to assist her. She had set up a bookkeeping system and prepared a thorough report showing what she had done to meet the state requirements.

"You should be hearin' something soon from that committee, Babe." George said confidently one day when Chessie wondered out loud if they would get their institutional license soon. She had complied with all the regulations and was just patiently waiting to hear from the worker in charge of her file.

Their anticipation turned to exhilaration when Chessie received notification by mail that beginning January 1, 1961,

Harris Home for Children was licensed to care for six girls and four boys between the ages of six and eighteen.

"I can't believe it," Chessie exclaimed. Having survived so many ups and downs, she smiled smugly to herself as she reread the words, *six girls and four boys between the ages of six and eighteen,* because by this time more than 142 different children had walked through the doors of their home, leaving residues of their little lives on her family's hearts. But at long last the difficult struggle to develop a legally-recognized institution for children reached fulfillment.

As Chessie sat in her brown leather rocker that evening thinking, she felt a tremendous satisfaction. There were so many children helped. She thought of Kate, the girl who had been diagnosed retarded, but after loving care and encouragement, the girl graduated from high school, became a baptized Christian, and was now holding down a good job.

In her mind's eye, she saw the children's faces and heard their voices as they responded to her instructions on manners, dating, and God. She remembered the birthday celebrations once a month and thought of the hours spent on her knees, receiving power from "the Man above."

As the memories flooded her mind, her face broke into a thankful smile when she thought of her wonderful God-given husband and children—always willing to give up conveniences, personal resources, and personal pleasure to do for someone else.

Then her mind propelled her into the future. How would they continue to manage? What about the many children still needing help? And what about more housing? What did the future hold?

Chapter 15

Changes

I will extol thee, my God, O king; and I will bless thy name for ever and ever (Psalm 145:1).

Twenty-one years sped by. The Harrises now parented as many as forty youngsters and teenagers at a time. Chessie continued to raise funds until she had six satellite homes and two dormitory-style buildings. The children lived in groups of five or six with resident adults.

The parenting was always demanding and sometimes frustrating. Many of the youngsters came from difficult family situations. Because of the mountains of paperwork and business to attend to, Chessie and George now spent most of their time in administration and fund raising.

On the evening of January 27, 1980, Chessie attended a United Way banquet. As a recipient of community money, she sought to be visible and involved—expressing appreciation by her presence at public functions.

As the evening's activities progressed, she became deeply moved at the incredible truth that Harris Home was a reality! In spite of racism, prejudice, and lean times, the dream she'd cherished for over forty years seemed almost fulfilled. Their facilities remained debt free—for that she was exceedingly thankful. However, lack of perpetual funding continually nagged at her conscientiousness.

"We've come a long way, Lord." Chessie's thoughts reached automatically to her Father in heaven. "But I am so tired!" At seventy-four, Chessie was beginning to feel the physical strain of years of hard labor.

As the banquet proceeded and she finished her meal, Chessie began to feel odd. After attacks of angina for the past four years, she didn't anticipate any more health problems. But she felt slightly dizzy, and had pains in her arms and chest.

The symptoms intensified and Chessie began praying, "Lord, don't let Satan take advantage of this situation. What should I do?" A small voice seemed to whisper, "Go to the car."

Chessie got up from the table, left the room quietly, feeling like at any moment she might faint. Stumbling to her trusty Buick, she got in, turned the key, and kept praying.

"Lord, just let me get home—let me get to Papa."

The old car seemed to know just where to go, and after what seemed like an eternity, she pulled in the driveway. With great effort she managed to drag herself into the house. George looked up in surprise as she came in the front door.

"What's the matter?" he asked.

"I think maybe we ought to get in touch with the doctor," she whispered, by this time barely able to talk.

George hurried to the phone and called Chester, who lived a few blocks away. Within a half hour, father and son had Chessie at the hospital emergency room.

"This lady must go to intensive care immediately," the physician commanded with urgency in his voice, as he assisted two aids who placed her on a cart. Quickly they disappeared behind two large doors at the end of a long hall.

After what seemed an agonizingly long time, the doctor appeared and said to George, "Mr. Harris, your wife's having another heart attack." George's own heart seemed to jump to his throat as he thought, "How will she survive this one? It's her fourth!"

But survive Chessie did. Although she was in intensive care for six weeks, she and God had a wonderful time together.

"I have so many questions and concerns about my children and the future of Harris Home," she prayed constantly. Yet, while a prisoner in her hospital bed, she experienced a closeness to God outweighing any previous encounter.

A month and two weeks after her fourth heart attack, Chessie came home. Her orders were to "take it easy for a year."

"I'll have to resign as director of Harris Home." Chessie's heart felt heavy as she verbalized her decision to George. "Who in the world will take my place?"

"We'll pray about it, Honey. God will send somebody," George encouraged.

As they had always done, Chessie and George laid their concerns in the lap of the Lord. They prayed earnestly that God would send a capable administrator to take Chessie's place.

About that time, Barbara Lloyd, a single mother, felt the Lord calling her. When she heard about the need at Harris Home, she immediately recognized this as a God-sent opportunity for service. Leaving a lucrative position in the East, she called Chessie and said, "I'll come and take care of your children for you."

The change in administration presented many challenges. But Barbara forged ahead while Chessie recuperated. Although she was not now actually involved in running Harris Home, Chessie kept abreast of all that was happening, and her mind turned constantly.

"We must find a solid base of perpetual support," she said to George one evening as they sat on the porch of their red-brick home. "Harris Home is almost like a neglected child itself," she continued. "It's an orphan. The Harris family brought it into existence—it's not supported by any religious groups or government agencies. There's no parent body—only Harris family. And as long as we live, we *must* continue to search for permanent funding." Her heart felt heavy with concern as she pondered the Home's financial future.

"I'll continue to trust in You and follow Your plan, Lord," she prayed, after George had gone back in the house, "because there's still so much to be done for children." After a few more moments of silent meditation, Chessie felt a familiar peace. She relinquished her concerns to God. She realized she had much for which to praise His name—a competent, professional staff to run Harris Home, and the case histories of over 900 "reclaimed kids" who had passed through their doors and had grown up to become doctors, farmers, businessmen, and homemakers. Only a few had ever been in trouble, and of her own children, three had master's degrees in social work and one now worked at Harris Home.

Thinking on her blessings, Chessie's mind turned to George, her faithful companion and loyal supporter. Without his love for her and all the children who had passed through their lives, she knew she could never have done what she did. And she couldn't forget the promise she made to God so long before in the cornfield. The promise to help children feel good about themselves.

Chessie pondered the bitter road of prejudice she and others like her had trodden. And she renewed her determination to rebuild the unjust world of bigotry and hatred. Clenching her fist in renewal, she thought what her color had cost her and millions of other blacks throughout history.

She closed her eyes and surrendered herself to the vivid memories of long ago. She'd come a long way as an eager sharecropper's daughter from the poverty and depression of "Little Texas." The comforting words of a favorite hymn came to memory:

> Through many dangers, toils, and snares,
>   I have already come;
> 'Tis grace hath brought me safe thus far,
>   And grace will lead me home.

Her thoughts raced faster and faster as she chose to shake off the apprehension about a secure financial future for Harris Home and the needy children yet to come. As she gave her future agenda of needs to the Lord, her uneasiness subsided.

"I don't know where the money's coming from for future funding, but God will take care of it," she thought to herself. After all, hadn't God always kept His promise to her in the past? She would give Him her future as well.

Epilogue

Huntsville, Alabama—May 15, 1984.

Her dark brown face is unlined. Intense gray eyes make contact as she talks. Standing a little under five feet, four inches, Chessie Harris, seventy-eight still moves quickly. She's just arrived with her husband George of 53 years at the Von Braun Civic Center West Exhibit Hall. The Harris family is about to enjoy a thirtieth anniversary banquet in honor of three decades of caring for Alabama's destitute children.

Dressed in a simple yellow formal, Chessie graciously accepts a white orchid and helps Papa pin on his boutonniere.

"Madlyn, has the photographer arrived yet?"

"I haven't seen him," I answer as we move together through the sifting mass of bodies toward our reserved seats. Throughout the huge room, little groups of people talk and laugh. Silk dresses, furs, and Botany 500 suits indicate a glittering social occasion.

I follow Chessie as she graciously greets people. We stop as she says hello to a group of young black boys dressed in suits and ties. Chessie calls them "some of my other children." Their earnest eyes follow her every move, and they all call her "Mama Harris."

Thumbing through the professionally printed booklet as we

continue toward our table, I'm surprised to see so many pres-
tigious names jump out at me. Doctor Henry Bradford, Mayor
Joe R. Davis, and Father George R. Clements. My mind
turned inward. Ah, yes. I'd seen Father Clements on television
several times. He's the first black graduate of Chicago's
Quigley Seminary. He founded the One Church, One Child
program to promote the adoption of black children in the
Chicago area.

My eyes turn once again toward Chessie. She eases comfor-
tably through the cream of Huntsville society. Exuding confidence, she radiates love and concern for all.

I observe her carefully. Her large hands reach out often to
touch. And she doesn't forget George. She touches his arm
often. I can't help thinking how uncomfortable he seems in his
black suit, white lace evening shirt, and bow tie.

"Isn't this something?" Chessie points with pleasure to the
raised stage where there are two tiers of banquet tables. On
the main floor, the large hall is filled with tables for six, veiled
with cascading white linen cloths. Behind us, TV cameras follow the scene. Chessie stops for a moment, making a statement to the impatient press.

As she talks, my mind recalls the many names she'd been
called—"Miracle Worker of Alabama," a "nice hustler," and of
course the familiar "Mama Harris." Time has not mellowed
her drive. Joy and tranquility erupt spontaneously.

At last we are seated—Chessie and George up on the stage,
and I down on the main floor in front. The room is filled now.
This audience, a flower garden of excited faces, exudes respect
for Mrs. George Harris. This most proper social occasion
would have caused her slave ancestors a great deal of
astonishment and delight. The distinguished group gathered
this evening seem to melt the racial and religious boundaries
prevalent in times past in this part of the South.

As introductions precede dinner, waitresses in black skirts
and white blouses carry trays of steaming hot food.

After dinner an impressive program begins. In Chessie's
face I detect mixed emotions as she listens intently to the
many tributes and honors. I think of her reluctance to be

depicted as others see her. This is probably the largest hurdle in writing her story. She is so modest, so lacking in self-serving motivation that she seems, at times, unreal.

My mind recalls the many honors and tributes she's received recently, not the least of which is a letter of congratulations from President Ronald Reagan. As she enters her fourth decade of caring, she has lost track of the numerous awards and honors she and Harris Home have received.

But the people involved in Harris Home and the ones she's helped will never forget. Harris Home is now a privately-owned, foster care agency for both the Huntsville area and the state of Alabama. It includes a professional staff, provides child care, counseling, and other social and enrichment programs for children of the state. And this evening, ironically, some of the agencies who initially stifled her progress are represented here and are applauding her outstanding accomplishments and cheering her future endeavors.

This amazing woman clawed her way through the serious problems of a country embroiled in prejudice and racial hatred. She dared to challenge the bureaucratic state welfare system, and she succeeded in founding the first home for neglected black children in Alabama.

She's come a long way—that chubby little girl with sparkling brown eyes and determined will. She and her husband George have invested heavily in others and have the joy of seeing unloved children's eyes light up with the joy of acceptance.

One of my favorite authors sums up Chessie's life beautifully:

"God did not design that His wonderful plan to redeem men should achieve only insignificant results. All who will go to work, trusting not in what they themselves can do, but in what God can do for and through them, will certainly realize the fulfillment of His promise" (*The Desire of Ages*, p. 667).

Chessie's promise to God will ever be in the forefront of her mind. Until her productive life is over, she will ever search for ways to fulfill God's plan for her life. And because of her dedication, her love will ever remain in the hearts of the children she has helped.

Above: Chessie and George in the early 60s with the children in front of the first "Harris Home." Today, seven cottages house more than forty children.

Left: Chessie as she appears today at eighty-two years of age.

Left: George Wallace, former Governor of Alabama, signs proclammation declaring January 16, 1978 "Chessie Harris Day."

George Ernest Harris
January 17, 1895—August 4, 1988

During the preparation of this book, we were saddened to learn of the passing of George Harris on August 4, 1988. He was ninety-three.

At the same time, Chessie was hospitalized for her second open-heart surgery. Against her physician's protests, Chessie attended her loving companion's funeral at the Oakwood College church, in spite of having to be transported by ambulance.

Out of profound respect for this husband, father, and man of God, we wish to close this book with two of the many tributes to George written by close friends and associates privileged to have known and loved "Pop" Harris.

—The editors

> Often unheralded and unsung, in his undemonstrative and unassuming manner, [George] was constantly engaged in fixing and sharing, guiding and caring. . . . Jesus Christ reminds us that he who would be great in the kingdom must serve. Indeed, a great man is what he is because of what he does. George Harris was a great man.
>
> —Henry Bradford, Jr.
> Former president of the Harris Home Board of Directors

> Christened George Ernest Harris at birth, [he] was affectionately known to his children—natural, adopted and spiritual—as well as all others who were close to him as "Pop." . . . His pertinacious faith in his Lord sustained him through the valleys and over the mountains of his life and inspired all who were touched by him. Pop, "tomorrow is the new moon, thou shalt be missed because thy seat shall be empty." 1 Samuel 20:18.
>
> —Don & Vera Blake
> Family friends

At the time of this writing, Chessie, eighty-two, is recovering nicely from her heart surgery and is fully convinced that God has more work for her to do. A special thanks to Marilyn Mabry, the Harris's eldest daughter and secretary to The Harris Family Foundation, Inc., for her help with this tribute page.